The Ultimate Pastry Cookbook

Dishes, Volume 7

Olivia Bennett

Published by B&H Publishing Group, 2025.

While every precaution has been taken in the preparation of this book, the publisher assumes no responsibility for errors or omissions, or for damages resulting from the use of the information contained herein.

THE ULTIMATE PASTRY COOKBOOK

First edition. February 23, 2025.

Copyright © 2025 Olivia Bennett.

ISBN: 979-8230717744

Written by Olivia Bennett.

Table of Contents

To the passionate bakers, the curious beginners, and everyone who finds joy in the art of pastry—this book is for you.

To my family and friends, whose love and encouragement have filled my kitchen with warmth, laughter, and countless taste tests.

And to all who believe that a flaky crust, a delicate tart, or a perfectly puffed pastry can bring people together—may your ovens stay warm, your doughs rise beautifully, and your creations always be shared with love.

Introduction: The Art and Science of Pastry

Pastry-making is a timeless art that weaves together tradition, precision, and creativity. From the delicate, buttery layers of a croissant to the tender, flaky crust of a fruit tart, pastries are a celebration of craftsmanship and culinary innovation. They evoke comfort, joy, and a sense of indulgence, transcending borders and uniting cultures through a shared love for these delectable creations.

In this chapter, we will explore the rich history of pastry-making across cultures, delve into the delicate balance between precision and creativity required for pastry success, and provide an overview of the essential tools, techniques, and ingredients that will serve as the foundation for the recipes in this book.

The History of Pastry-Making Across Cultures

The story of pastry-making is as old as civilization itself, with roots in ancient Egypt, Greece, and Rome. Over the centuries, pastries have evolved, shaped by cultural influences and the availability of ingredients, into the diverse and sophisticated creations we know today.

1. Ancient Origins

- Egyptian Beginnings: Pastry-making can be traced back to ancient Egypt, where cooks used a basic dough made of flour and water to create simple pastries. Honey and nuts were often added to sweeten these early treats.

- Greek and Roman Innovations: The Greeks introduced filo dough, characterized by its thin, delicate layers, while the Romans expanded the use of pastries in both savory and sweet dishes, incorporating fruits, nuts, and cheese.

2. The Middle Ages

- During the medieval period, pastries became a symbol of wealth and status, with intricate pies and tarts gracing the tables of European nobility.

- Spices such as cinnamon and nutmeg, introduced through trade routes, added depth and complexity to pastry recipes.

3. The French Renaissance

- France emerged as a hub for pastry innovation during the Renaissance. Bakers refined techniques for puff pastry and choux pastry, laying the groundwork for iconic desserts such as éclairs and mille-feuille.

- Pastry schools and guilds flourished, elevating the craft to an esteemed art form.

4. Global Influence and Modern Pastries

- The spread of European colonization introduced pastries to new regions, where they were adapted to incorporate local ingredients and flavors.

- Today, pastries reflect the rich tapestry of global cuisine, from Middle Eastern baklava to Latin American empanadas and Japanese mochi pastries.

The Balance Between Precision and Creativity

Pastry-making is often described as a science and an art, requiring both technical skill and a flair for creativity. Achieving this balance is essential to mastering the craft.

1. The Role of Precision

- Measurements Matter: Pastry recipes rely on precise measurements to achieve the desired texture and structure. A slight variation in ingredient ratios can drastically alter the outcome.

- Temperature Control: From the temperature of the butter in puff pastry to the baking temperature of choux, precision ensures consistent results.

- Timing is Key: Overmixing dough or underbaking a crust can lead to disappointing results, highlighting the importance of timing in pastry-making.

2. The Role of Creativity

- Flavor Pairings: Experimenting with unique flavor combinations, such as lavender and lemon or chocolate and chili, allows bakers to create memorable pastries.

- Aesthetic Appeal: Decorative techniques, including latticework, glazing, and stenciling, transform pastries into visual masterpieces.

- Personal Touch: Creativity shines through in the adaptation of classic recipes to suit individual tastes or dietary preferences.

3. Striking the Balance

- Successful pastry-making requires a foundation of technical knowledge, which serves as a canvas for creative expression.

- As you gain confidence in the fundamentals, you'll find opportunities to infuse your personality and style into your creations.

Essential Tools, Techniques, and Ingredients

To embark on your pastry-making journey, you'll need a well-equipped kitchen, a mastery of fundamental techniques, and a thorough understanding of key ingredients.

1. Essential Tools

- Rolling Pin: A versatile tool for rolling out dough to the perfect thickness.

- Pastry Cutter: Ideal for shaping dough and creating decorative edges.

- Silicone Baking Mats: Provide a non-stick surface for rolling and baking pastries.

- Pastry Brush: Used for applying glazes, egg washes, and butter.

- Piping Bags and Tips: Essential for filling éclairs, decorating tarts, and piping choux pastry.

- Pastry Blender: Simplifies the process of cutting butter into flour for crusts.

- Pie Weights: Ensure even baking of crusts by preventing puffing.

2. Fundamental Techniques

- Mixing Dough: Achieving the right balance of flour, fat, and liquid is crucial for a tender crust.

- Lamination: The process of folding and rolling butter into dough to create layers in puff pastry.

- Blind Baking: Pre-baking a crust to prevent sogginess when adding wet fillings.

- Piping: A technique for shaping and filling choux pastry, cream, and other elements.

- Glazing and Decorating: Adding the finishing touches that enhance both flavor and presentation.

3. Key Ingredients

- Flour: The backbone of pastry, with different types (all-purpose, bread, cake, gluten-free) offering unique properties.

- Butter: Provides richness and flakiness, with European-style butter offering higher fat content for superior results.

- Eggs: Essential for binding, leavening, and adding richness to pastry dough and fillings.

- Sugar: Adds sweetness and enhances browning.

- Liquid: Water, milk, or cream, used to bind dough and add moisture.

- Flavorings: Vanilla, almond extract, citrus zest, and spices elevate the taste of pastries.

What This Book Offers

This book is your comprehensive guide to mastering pastry-making, whether you're a novice baker or an experienced pâtissier. Here's what you can expect:

1. Step-by-Step Instructions
    - Clear, detailed guidance for each recipe ensures success, even for complex pastries.
    2. A Diverse Range of Recipes
    - From sweet to savory, classic to modern, this book covers the full spectrum of pastry-making.
    3. Tips and Tricks
    - Troubleshooting advice and expert tips help you avoid common pitfalls and refine your technique.
    4. Creative Inspiration
    - Suggestions for flavor variations, decorative techniques, and themed pastries spark your creativity.

A Final Note

As you embark on this journey, remember that pastry-making is as much about the process as it is about the result. Embrace the challenges, celebrate your successes, and don't be afraid to experiment. This book is here to guide you every step of the way, equipping you with the knowledge and confidence to create pastries that delight both the eye and the palate.

Let's roll up our sleeves, dust our workstations with flour, and dive into the wonderful world of pastry. Your adventure begins now!

Chapter 1: Understanding Pastry Doughs

The foundation of any great pastry lies in the dough. Pastry doughs are as varied as the creations they form, each offering unique textures, flavors, and applications. From the sturdy shortcrust that holds a rich quiche to the ethereal layers of puff pastry, the versatility of dough is a testament to the artistry of pastry-making.

In this chapter, we will explore the differences between the most common types of pastry dough—shortcrust, puff, choux, filo, and phyllo—along with tips for mastering the basics. By understanding their unique characteristics, you'll be able to choose the perfect dough for your next pastry project.

1. The Five Essential Pastry Doughs

Shortcrust Pastry

Shortcrust pastry, also known as pâte brisée in French, is a versatile dough prized for its tender, crumbly texture. It is often used for pies, tarts, and quiches, providing a neutral base that complements both sweet and savory fillings.

Characteristics:

- Texture: Tender and crumbly, with a slight flakiness.
    - Flavor: Buttery and mild, making it a perfect canvas for bold fillings.
    - Structure: Sturdy enough to hold wet fillings without becoming soggy.

When to Use:

- Sweet tarts like lemon or chocolate ganache.
    - Savory dishes such as quiches or pot pies.

Key Techniques:

1. Cold Ingredients: Ensure that butter and liquids are cold to prevent the fat from melting before baking.

2. Minimal Handling: Overworking the dough can develop gluten, resulting in a tough crust.

3. Blind Baking: Pre-baking the crust with pie weights ensures it stays crisp when filled.

Puff Pastry

Puff pastry, or pâte feuilletée, is a laminated dough made by layering butter and dough through a process of folding and rolling. When baked, the butter creates steam, causing the dough to puff into hundreds of delicate, flaky layers.

Characteristics:

- Texture: Light, airy, and crisp, with distinct layers.
- Flavor: Rich and buttery.
- Structure: Fragile and tender, making it ideal for lighter fillings.

When to Use:

- Sweet pastries like palmiers or turnovers.
- Savory appetizers such as vol-au-vents or cheese straws.

Key Techniques:

1. Chill Between Folds: Keeping the dough cold ensures the butter stays solid and layers remain intact.

2. Roll Evenly: Consistent thickness is crucial for even puffing during baking.

3. High Heat: Bake at a high temperature (375–400°F) to create steam and achieve maximum puff.

Choux Pastry

Choux pastry, or pâte à choux, is a unique dough made by cooking flour, butter, and water on the stovetop before adding eggs. It relies on steam for leavening, creating hollow centers perfect for fillings.

Characteristics:

- Texture: Crisp exterior with a soft, airy interior.
    - Flavor: Mild, allowing fillings to take center stage.
    - Structure: Hollow, ideal for piped or spooned fillings.

When to Use:

- Desserts like éclairs, cream puffs, or profiteroles.
    - Savory options such as gougères (cheese puffs).

Key Techniques:

1. Cook the Dough: Properly cook the dough on the stovetop to eliminate excess moisture before adding eggs.
    2. Add Eggs Gradually: Incorporate eggs one at a time to achieve the right consistency—smooth, glossy, and pipeable.
    3. Steam for Rise: Bake in a preheated oven with a source of steam for optimal puffing.

Filo Dough

Filo, or phyllo, dough is a paper-thin pastry made from flour, water, and oil. Unlike other doughs, filo is used in layers, often brushed with butter or oil between each sheet to create crisp, flaky results.

Characteristics:

- Texture: Shatteringly crisp and delicate.
    - Flavor: Neutral, allowing fillings to shine.

- Structure: Fragile when raw, but strong when layered and baked.

When to Use:

- Sweet dishes like baklava.
  - Savory options such as spanakopita or meat pies.

Key Techniques:

1. Work Quickly: Filo dries out rapidly, so keep unused sheets covered with a damp towel.
   2. Butter Generously: Brushing each layer with butter ensures crisp, golden results.
   3. Cut Before Baking: Scoring the dough prevents breakage when slicing after baking.

Phyllo Dough

Phyllo dough is often confused with filo dough due to its similar name and appearance. While both are thin and used in layered applications, phyllo dough is slightly thicker and more elastic, making it easier to handle.

Characteristics:

- Texture: Similar to filo but with a bit more chew.
  - Flavor: Neutral, with a hint of elasticity.
  - Structure: Stronger and less prone to tearing than filo.

When to Use:

- Layered dishes like strudels or savory turnovers.

Key Techniques:

1. Gentle Handling: Phyllo dough is delicate but forgiving, so handle with care.

2. Layer Strategically: Use fewer layers for lighter pastries or more for added structure.

How to Choose the Right Dough for Your Recipe

1. Consider Texture and Flavor

- For rich, buttery results, choose puff pastry.
    - For a sturdy base, opt for shortcrust.
    - For light, airy pastries, go with choux.

2. Match the Dough to the Filling

- Delicate fillings pair well with filo or phyllo.
    - Hearty, robust fillings need the support of shortcrust or puff pastry.

3. Think About Presentation

- Puff pastry and filo create dramatic, layered appearances.
    - Shortcrust offers a more understated, rustic look.

Tips for Mastering the Basics

1. Use High-Quality Ingredients
    - Choose unsalted butter for better flavor control.
    - Use unbleached, high-protein flour for structure and elasticity.
    2. Control the Temperature
    - Cold ingredients and work surfaces prevent the dough from becoming greasy or sticky.
    3. Practice Patience
    - Resting dough allows gluten to relax and improves texture.
    - Lamination requires time, but the results are worth it.
    4. Learn to Troubleshoot
    - Cracking dough: Add a small amount of liquid or rest it longer.
    - Soggy crusts: Blind bake or use a thicker dough layer.

Conclusion

Mastering pastry doughs is the first step toward creating a world of delicious possibilities. Each dough—shortcrust, puff, choux, filo, and phyllo—brings its own unique qualities to the table, offering endless opportunities for creativity and expression. By understanding their differences and practicing the fundamental techniques outlined in this chapter, you'll be well on your way to becoming a confident and versatile pastry chef. Let's dive deeper into the specific recipes and applications in the next chapter: "Perfecting Shortcrust Pastry."

Chapter 2: Essential Tools for Pastry Success

Pastry-making is an art that requires precision, creativity, and the right tools. A well-equipped kitchen not only makes the process smoother but also ensures consistent results. Whether you're crafting delicate puff pastry or sturdy shortcrust, having the proper tools at your disposal can elevate your pastry-making skills from amateur to professional.

In this chapter, we will explore the must-have tools for pastry-making, how to set up an efficient and organized workstation, and tips for maintaining and caring for your tools. By the end, you'll have the knowledge to equip your kitchen for pastry success.

Must-Have Equipment for Pastry-Making

Investing in high-quality pastry tools is essential for achieving professional results. Below is a comprehensive list of equipment and their uses in pastry-making.

1. Rolling Pins

A rolling pin is one of the most fundamental tools in a pastry chef's arsenal. Choosing the right one depends on the type of pastry you're making.

- Classic Wooden Rolling Pin: A versatile choice, ideal for rolling out most types of dough. Look for one with a smooth surface to prevent sticking.

- French Rolling Pin: Tapered at the ends, this pin offers greater control and precision for delicate doughs like puff pastry.

- Marble Rolling Pin: Excellent for maintaining a cool temperature, making it ideal for butter-based doughs like pie crusts and croissants.

- Non-Stick Rolling Pin: Coated with a non-stick surface, this pin is great for sticky doughs such as shortcrust.

2. Pastry Cutters

Pastry cutters are indispensable for shaping dough, creating decorative edges, and cutting even portions.

- Round Cutters: Perfect for cookies, biscuits, and individual tart shells.

- Fluted Cutters: Add a decorative touch to pie crusts and cookies.

- Wheel Cutter: Ideal for cutting straight or lattice patterns in pastry dough.

3. Silicone Baking Mats

Silicone mats provide a non-stick surface for rolling and baking pastry. They are reusable, easy to clean, and prevent dough from sticking to countertops.

- Benefits: Reduce the need for excess flour, ensuring a more tender pastry.

- Uses: Rolling out dough, lining baking sheets, and even baking delicate pastries like meringues.

4. Pastry Brushes

Pastry brushes are essential for applying egg washes, glazes, and melted butter.

- Natural Bristle Brushes: Offer a soft touch for delicate applications.

- Silicone Brushes: Durable and easy to clean, perfect for thicker applications like barbecue sauce or melted chocolate.

5. Piping Bags and Tips

Piping bags and tips are crucial for shaping choux pastry, decorating tarts, and filling éclairs.

- Reusable Piping Bags: Eco-friendly and durable, ideal for heavy-duty use.

- Disposable Piping Bags: Convenient for quick tasks or multiple colors of icing.

- Assorted Tips: Include round, star, and petal tips for versatility in decoration.

6. Pastry Blender

A pastry blender simplifies the process of cutting butter into flour, ensuring a tender, flaky crust.

- Benefits: Distributes fat evenly without warming it, maintaining the dough's integrity.

- Alternative: A fork or two knives can be used, but a pastry blender provides better control.

7. Pie Weights

Pie weights prevent crusts from puffing up during blind baking.
- Ceramic or Metal Weights: Reusable and easy to clean.
- Alternatives: Dried beans or rice can also be used as makeshift weights.

8. Cooling Racks

Cooling racks allow air to circulate around baked pastries, preventing sogginess and ensuring even cooling.
- Uses: Ideal for pies, cookies, and puff pastries.

9. Sharp Knives and Bench Scrapers

Precision cutting tools are vital for shaping dough and creating decorative elements.
- Sharp Knives: Perfect for clean cuts and intricate designs.
- Bench Scrapers: Versatile for portioning dough, lifting rolled-out pastry, and cleaning work surfaces.

10. Specialty Tools

- Lattice Roller: Creates intricate lattice patterns for pies.
- Dough Docker: Prevents air bubbles in pizza dough and puff pastry.
- Offset Spatula: Essential for spreading fillings and smoothing frosting.

Setting Up a Well-Organized Pastry-Making Station

An organized pastry-making station streamlines your workflow, ensuring efficiency and consistency. Here's how to set up your space for maximum productivity:

1. Designate a Pastry Zone

- Reserve a specific area in your kitchen for pastry-making.

- Ensure the surface is smooth and easy to clean, such as a marble or granite countertop.

2. Organize Tools by Function

- Store frequently used tools, like rolling pins and pastry cutters, within easy reach.

- Use drawers or bins to separate tools by category, such as cutting, rolling, and decorating.

3. Keep Ingredients Handy

- Store flour, sugar, and other dry ingredients in airtight containers.

- Refrigerate butter and other perishable items in an easily accessible spot.

4. Use a Cooling Area

- Designate a space for cooling racks, away from heat sources, to allow pastries to set properly.

5. Maintain a Clean Workspace

- Clean as you go to prevent clutter and cross-contamination.

- Use silicone mats or parchment paper to protect surfaces and simplify cleanup.

Maintenance and Care of Pastry Tools

Proper maintenance of your tools ensures their longevity and performance. Follow these tips to keep your equipment in top condition:

1. Cleaning

- Hand Wash Wooden Tools: Avoid soaking wooden rolling pins and pastry brushes to prevent warping.

- Dishwasher-Safe Items: Check manufacturer guidelines before placing tools in the dishwasher.

- Silicone Mats: Wash with warm soapy water and allow to air dry completely.

2. Storage

- Avoid Overcrowding: Store tools in a way that prevents damage, such as hanging rolling pins or using dividers for cutters.

- Protect Blades: Keep knives and bench scrapers in a knife block or protective sheath to maintain sharpness.

3. Regular Maintenance

- Sharpen Knives: Use a whetstone or knife sharpener to ensure clean cuts.

- Inspect Piping Bags: Check for wear and tear, replacing disposable bags as needed.

4. Seasonal Care

- If you bake seasonally, ensure tools are clean and dry before storing them for extended periods.

Tips for Success with Pastry Tools

1. Invest in Quality

- High-quality tools may cost more upfront but offer better performance and durability over time.

2. Start Simple

- Begin with the essentials, like a rolling pin, pastry cutter, and silicone mat. Add specialty tools as your skills advance.

3. Experiment

- Test different tools to find what works best for your style of pastry-making.

4. Practice

- Familiarize yourself with each tool through regular practice, building confidence and efficiency.

Conclusion

Mastering pastry-making begins with mastering your tools. From rolling pins and cutters to silicone mats and piping bags, each piece of equipment plays a vital role in creating beautiful and delicious pastries. By setting up an organized workspace and maintaining your tools with care, you'll set yourself up for success in every pastry project.

As we move forward, you'll build on this foundation by learning the specific techniques required for crafting different types of dough, fillings, and decorations. Let's continue this journey with the next chapter: *"Perfecting Shortcrust Pastry."*

Chapter 3: Perfecting Shortcrust Pastry

Shortcrust pastry, known for its tender, crumbly texture, is a cornerstone of baking. Whether used as a base for a sweet tart, a savory quiche, or a decadent chocolate creation, mastering this versatile dough is a vital skill for any baker. In this chapter, we will dive deep into the art of shortcrust pastry, exploring techniques to achieve the perfect texture, step-by-step recipes for different variations, and solutions to common issues like shrinking and cracking.

What Makes Shortcrust Pastry Unique?

Shortcrust pastry is prized for its balance of structure and tenderness. Unlike puff pastry, it doesn't rely on layers for its texture. Instead, its crumbly nature is achieved by incorporating fat into flour, creating a dough that holds its shape while remaining delicate.

Key Characteristics of Shortcrust Pastry

1. Tender Texture: Achieved through minimal gluten development.
   2. Versatility: Suitable for both sweet and savory applications.
   3. Ease of Preparation: Requires basic ingredients and simple techniques.

Techniques for Achieving a Tender, Flaky Crust

Achieving the perfect shortcrust pastry requires attention to detail at every stage of preparation. Here are the essential techniques:

1. Keep Ingredients Cold
   - Use chilled butter, ice-cold water, and even refrigerate your mixing bowl.
   - Cold ingredients prevent the fat from melting too quickly, maintaining distinct pockets of fat that create flakiness.
   2. Use the Right Flour
   - Choose low-protein flours, such as all-purpose or pastry flour, to minimize gluten development.
   - Avoid bread flour, which can make the crust tough.
   3. Incorporate Fat Properly

- Cut the fat (butter, shortening, or lard) into the flour until the mixture resembles coarse breadcrumbs.

- Aim for a mix of small and pea-sized fat pieces to achieve a balance of tenderness and flakiness.

4. Add Liquid Gradually

- Use just enough cold water to bring the dough together.

- Adding too much liquid can make the dough sticky and difficult to work with.

5. Handle the Dough Gently

- Avoid overmixing or kneading the dough, as this can activate gluten and result in a tough crust.

- Press the dough together lightly to form a cohesive ball.

6. Chill the Dough

- Rest the dough in the refrigerator for at least 30 minutes before rolling.

- Chilling helps relax gluten, firm up the fat, and prevent shrinkage during baking.

7. Roll Evenly

- Roll the dough on a lightly floured surface to an even thickness of about 1/8 inch.

- Turn the dough frequently to prevent sticking and ensure uniform thickness.

8. Blind Bake for Crispness

- Pre-bake the crust for tarts or pies with wet fillings.

- Use pie weights or dried beans to prevent the crust from puffing up during baking.

Shortcrust Pastry Recipes

Let's explore three variations of shortcrust pastry: classic sweet crust, savory crust, and indulgent chocolate crust. Each recipe is tailored to specific uses, but they all share the same foundational techniques.

1. Sweet Shortcrust Pastry

Perfect for desserts like fruit tarts, custard pies, and sweet galettes.

Ingredients:

- 2 1/2 cups (315 g) all-purpose flour
    - 1/4 cup (50 g) granulated sugar
    - 1/2 teaspoon salt
    - 1 cup (225 g) unsalted butter, chilled and cubed
    - 4–5 tablespoons ice water

Instructions:

1. Combine Dry Ingredients:
    - In a large bowl, mix flour, sugar, and salt.
    2. Incorporate Butter:
    - Cut in the chilled butter using a pastry blender or your fingertips until the mixture resembles coarse crumbs.
    3. Add Water Gradually:
    - Sprinkle in ice water, one tablespoon at a time, mixing gently until the dough just comes together.
    4. Form and Chill:
    - Shape the dough into a disc, wrap it in plastic wrap, and refrigerate for at least 30 minutes.
    5. Roll Out and Bake:
    - Roll out the dough, fit it into a tart pan, and trim the edges. Blind bake at 375°F (190°C) for 15–20 minutes or until golden.

2. Savory Shortcrust Pastry

Ideal for quiches, pot pies, and savory galettes.

Ingredients:

- 2 1/2 cups (315 g) all-purpose flour
    - 1 teaspoon salt
    - 1/2 teaspoon black pepper (optional)
    - 1 cup (225 g) unsalted butter, chilled and cubed

- 4–6 tablespoons ice water

Instructions:

1. Combine Dry Ingredients:
   - In a bowl, mix flour, salt, and pepper.
   2. Incorporate Butter:
   - Cut in the butter until the mixture resembles coarse crumbs.
   3. Add Water Gradually:
   - Mix in ice water, one tablespoon at a time, until the dough comes together.
   4. Form and Chill:
   - Shape the dough into a disc, wrap it, and refrigerate for at least 30 minutes.
   5. Roll Out and Bake:
   - Roll the dough to fit your pie or tart pan. Pre-bake for quiches or fill directly for pot pies.

3. Chocolate Shortcrust Pastry

A decadent base for chocolate tarts, cream pies, and indulgent desserts.

Ingredients:

- 2 cups (250 g) all-purpose flour
   - 1/4 cup (25 g) cocoa powder
   - 1/2 cup (100 g) granulated sugar
   - 1/2 teaspoon salt
   - 1 cup (225 g) unsalted butter, chilled and cubed
   - 4–5 tablespoons ice water

Instructions:

1. Combine Dry Ingredients:
   - In a bowl, whisk together flour, cocoa powder, sugar, and salt.
   2. Incorporate Butter:

- Cut in the butter until the mixture resembles coarse crumbs.

3. Add Water Gradually:

- Mix in ice water until the dough just comes together.

4. Form and Chill:

- Shape the dough into a disc, wrap it, and refrigerate for at least 30 minutes.

5. Roll Out and Bake:

- Roll the dough and fit it into your tart pan. Blind bake as needed for your recipe.

Troubleshooting Common Issues

Even experienced bakers encounter challenges with shortcrust pastry. Here's how to address the most common problems:

1. Shrinking Crust

- Cause: Overworking the dough or insufficient chilling.

- Solution: Handle the dough minimally and always chill before baking. Avoid stretching the dough when fitting it into the pan.

2. Cracking Dough

- Cause: Dough is too dry or too cold.

- Solution: Add a teaspoon of water at a time to moisten dry dough. Allow chilled dough to rest at room temperature for a few minutes before rolling.

3. Soggy Bottom

- Cause: Wet fillings or underbaking.

- Solution: Blind bake the crust with pie weights and brush with an egg wash to create a moisture barrier.

4. Tough Texture

- Cause: Overmixing or using high-protein flour.

- Solution: Use a gentle hand and low-protein flour for tender results.

Conclusion

Mastering shortcrust pastry is a rewarding endeavor that opens the door to countless culinary creations. By focusing on the techniques outlined in this chapter, experimenting with the provided recipes, and learning to troubleshoot common issues, you'll gain the confidence to craft pies, tarts, and quiches that are as visually stunning as they are delicious.

In the next chapter, we'll delve into the world of puff pastry, exploring the art of lamination and the secrets behind creating those beautifully layered, buttery treats. Let's continue the journey!

Chapter 4: The Magic of Puff Pastry

Puff pastry, or pâte feuilletée, is often regarded as one of the most sophisticated and rewarding pastry types. Its hallmark lies in its ethereal layers—light, crisp, and buttery—created through the intricate process of lamination. While it might seem daunting, mastering puff pastry is entirely achievable with patience, precision, and a solid understanding of the techniques involved.

In this chapter, we'll explore the magic behind lamination, provide detailed recipes for classic puff pastry and its quicker cousin, rough puff pastry, and guide you through the essential steps of folding, chilling, and rolling. With practice, you'll be equipped to create stunning pastries, from flaky croissants to elegant mille-feuille.

Understanding Lamination: The Science Behind the Layers

What is Lamination?

Lamination is the process of creating layers of dough and butter by repeatedly folding and rolling them together. During baking, the water in the butter turns into steam, which separates the layers of dough, creating the light, flaky texture that defines puff pastry.

The Importance of Butter

Butter is the star of puff pastry, and its quality greatly impacts the final product.
- Plasticity: Butter must be pliable but not too soft, allowing it to spread evenly without breaking through the dough.
- High Fat Content: European-style butter, with a fat content of at least 82%, is ideal for puff pastry due to its lower water content.

The Role of Dough

The dough, known as détrempe, acts as the structural base for the butter layers.

- Elasticity: Achieved through gluten development, ensuring the dough can stretch without tearing.

- Moisture: A well-hydrated dough makes rolling and folding easier.

Key Steps in Lamination

1. Encasing the Butter: The butter is enclosed in the dough, forming a package known as the pâton.

2. Rolling and Folding: The pâton is rolled out and folded to create multiple layers.

3. Chilling: Between each fold, the dough is chilled to relax the gluten and keep the butter solid.

Recipes

1. Classic Puff Pastry

Ingredients:

- 2 1/2 cups (315 g) all-purpose flour
    - 1/2 teaspoon salt
    - 1/4 cup (60 ml) cold water
    - 1/4 cup (60 ml) cold milk
    - 1 cup (225 g) unsalted butter, chilled but pliable

Instructions:

1. Prepare the Dough (Détrempe):
    - In a large bowl, mix flour and salt. Add water and milk, mixing until the dough comes together. Knead lightly until smooth. Wrap and refrigerate for 30 minutes.
    2. Prepare the Butter Block (Beurrage):
    - Place the butter between two sheets of parchment paper. Pound and shape it into a 5x5-inch square. Chill until firm but pliable.
    3. Encasing the Butter:

- Roll the dough into an 8x8-inch square. Place the butter block diagonally in the center. Fold the corners of the dough over the butter, enclosing it completely. Pinch seams to seal.

4. First Roll and Fold (Single Fold):

- Roll the dough into a 10x20-inch rectangle. Fold the top third down and the bottom third up, like folding a letter. Rotate 90 degrees and chill for 30 minutes.

5. Second and Third Folds (Double Fold):

- Repeat the rolling and folding process twice more, chilling between folds.

6. Final Chill:

- Wrap the dough and refrigerate for at least 2 hours before using.

2. Rough Puff Pastry

Rough puff pastry is a quicker alternative to classic puff pastry, sacrificing some precision but still delivering excellent results.

Ingredients:

- 2 1/2 cups (315 g) all-purpose flour
    - 1 teaspoon salt
    - 1 cup (225 g) unsalted butter, cold and cubed
    - 2/3 cup (160 ml) ice water

Instructions:

1. Combine Ingredients:
    - In a bowl, mix flour and salt. Add the cold, cubed butter, tossing to coat.
    2. Add Water:
    - Gradually add ice water, mixing until the dough just comes together.
    3. Roll and Fold:
    - Roll the dough into a 10x20-inch rectangle. Fold the top third down and the bottom third up. Rotate 90 degrees and repeat 3–4 times, chilling between folds.
    4. Chill:

- Wrap the dough and refrigerate for 1 hour before using.

Step-by-Step Guide to Folding, Chilling, and Rolling

1. Rolling Out the Dough
   - Flour the Surface: Use a light dusting of flour to prevent sticking.
   - Even Pressure: Roll from the center outward, turning the dough frequently.
   2. Folding Techniques
   - Single Fold: Divide the dough visually into thirds, fold the top third down, and the bottom third up.
   - Double Fold: Divide the dough into quarters. Fold the top quarter down and the bottom quarter up to meet in the center, then fold in half like a book.
   3. Chilling Between Folds
   - Chill the dough for at least 30 minutes between folds to relax the gluten and firm up the butter.
   4. Final Rolling
   - Roll the dough to the desired thickness (usually 1/8 inch) before cutting and shaping.

Common Uses for Puff Pastry

1. Sweet Pastries
   - Palmiers: Rolled with sugar and baked until caramelized.
   - Fruit Tarts: Topped with custard and fresh fruit.
   - Napoleons: Layered with pastry cream and icing.
2. Savory Pastries
   - Vol-au-Vents: Hollow shells filled with savory fillings.

- Sausage Rolls: Wrapped around seasoned meat.
- Cheese Straws: Twisted with cheese and herbs.

Troubleshooting Common Issues

1. Butter Leaking
    - Cause: Butter softened too much during rolling.
    - Solution: Chill the dough thoroughly and ensure even butter distribution.

2. Uneven Puffing
    - Cause: Dough rolled unevenly or folded incorrectly.
    - Solution: Use even pressure and consistent folds.
    3. Tough Texture
    - Cause: Overworking the dough or using too much flour.
    - Solution: Handle the dough gently and use minimal flour for rolling.

Conclusion

The magic of puff pastry lies in its ability to transform simple ingredients into layers of light, buttery perfection. By understanding the science of lamination, practicing the folding and chilling techniques, and experimenting with classic and rough puff recipes, you'll develop the skills needed to create a wide range of exquisite pastries.

In the next chapter, we'll explore another cornerstone of pastry-making: *"Mastering Choux Pastry."* Let's continue this delicious journey!

Chapter 5: Mastering Choux Pastry

Choux pastry, or pâte à choux, is one of the most versatile and unique pastry doughs in the culinary world. Light, airy, and hollow, it serves as the foundation for both sweet and savory delights like éclairs, cream puffs, and gougères. Unlike other doughs, choux relies on steam rather than chemical leaveners to puff up, creating its signature texture and shape.

This chapter will delve into the science of steam and how it works in choux pastry, provide recipes for iconic choux creations, and offer tips for piping and shaping to achieve bakery-quality results.

The Science of Steam: How Choux Dough Puffs Up

Choux pastry's distinctive puff comes from a fascinating interplay of ingredients, technique, and heat. Here's how it works:

1. High Moisture Content

- Choux dough is unique in its high water content, contributed by water, milk, eggs, and butter.

- During baking, this moisture turns into steam, expanding the dough and creating the hollow interior.

2. Cooking the Dough

- Choux dough is cooked on the stovetop before baking. This step gelatinizes the starch in the flour, giving the dough its strength and elasticity.

- Cooking also removes excess moisture, ensuring the dough isn't too wet to hold its shape during piping.

3. Steam as a Leavener

- Unlike other doughs that rely on yeast or baking powder, choux pastry uses steam to rise.

- High oven heat creates an initial burst of steam, which puffs up the dough. As the structure sets, the outside becomes crisp while the inside remains airy and hollow.

4. The Role of Eggs

- Eggs play a crucial role in choux pastry, contributing moisture, structure, and richness.

- Properly incorporating eggs ensures the dough is smooth, glossy, and capable of trapping steam.

Recipes

Let's explore three classic recipes that showcase the versatility of choux pastry: éclairs, cream puffs, and gougères.

1. Éclairs

These elongated pastries are filled with pastry cream and topped with a glossy glaze, making them a favorite at pâtisseries worldwide.

Ingredients (Makes 12):

For the Choux Pastry:
- 1/2 cup (120 ml) water
- 1/2 cup (120 ml) whole milk
- 1/2 cup (115 g) unsalted butter
- 1/4 teaspoon salt
- 1 cup (125 g) all-purpose flour
- 4 large eggs

For the Filling:
- 2 cups pastry cream (see Chapter 9 for recipe)

For the Glaze:
- 1/2 cup (85 g) semisweet chocolate, melted
- 2 tablespoons heavy cream

Instructions:

1. Make the Dough:

- In a saucepan, combine water, milk, butter, and salt. Heat until the butter melts and the mixture comes to a boil.

- Remove from heat, add the flour all at once, and stir vigorously until a smooth dough forms. Return to low heat and cook for 2 minutes, stirring constantly, to remove excess moisture.

2. Incorporate the Eggs:

- Transfer the dough to a mixing bowl. Let cool slightly. Add the eggs one at a time, mixing well after each addition. The dough should be smooth, glossy, and pipeable.

3. Pipe the Éclairs:

- Preheat oven to 400°F (200°C). Line a baking sheet with parchment paper.

- Transfer the dough to a piping bag fitted with a large round tip. Pipe 4-inch logs onto the sheet, spacing them 2 inches apart.

4. Bake:

- Bake for 15 minutes, then reduce the temperature to 350°F (175°C) and bake for an additional 20 minutes until golden and crisp. Let cool completely.

5. Fill and Glaze:

- Use a skewer to poke a hole in each éclair. Fill a piping bag with pastry cream and pipe it into the éclairs.

- Mix melted chocolate with heavy cream and spread over the tops of the éclairs.

2. Cream Puffs

Light and airy, cream puffs are filled with whipped cream or custard and dusted with powdered sugar.

Ingredients (Makes 20):

For the Choux Pastry:
- Same as éclairs recipe

For the Filling:
- 2 cups heavy whipping cream
- 2 tablespoons powdered sugar
- 1 teaspoon vanilla extract

Instructions:

1. Make the Dough:
   - Follow the same process as for éclairs.
   2. Pipe the Puffs:
   - Preheat oven to 400°F (200°C). Line a baking sheet with parchment paper.
   - Pipe 1 1/2-inch mounds of dough onto the sheet, spacing them 2 inches apart.
   3. Bake:
   - Bake for 15 minutes at 400°F (200°C), then reduce the temperature to 350°F (175°C) and bake for another 15–20 minutes until golden. Let cool.
   4. Prepare the Filling:
   - Whip the cream, powdered sugar, and vanilla until stiff peaks form.
   5. Fill and Serve:
   - Slice the tops off the puffs, fill with whipped cream, and replace the tops. Dust with powdered sugar.

3. Gougères

These savory cheese puffs are perfect for appetizers or snacks.

Ingredients (Makes 24):

For the Choux Pastry:
   - Same as éclairs recipe, but omit milk and add 1/2 teaspoon black pepper.
   For the Cheese:
   - 1 cup (100 g) grated Gruyère or cheddar

Instructions:

1. Make the Dough:
   - Follow the same process as for éclairs, adding the cheese and pepper after the eggs are incorporated.
   2. Pipe the Gougères:

- Preheat oven to 375°F (190°C). Line a baking sheet with parchment paper.
- Pipe 1 1/2-inch mounds of dough onto the sheet.
3. Bake:
- Bake for 25–30 minutes until golden and puffed. Serve warm.

Tips for Piping and Achieving Consistent Shapes

1. Use the Right Piping Bag and Tip
- A reusable or disposable piping bag with a round or star tip works best for choux pastry.
2. Hold the Bag at the Correct Angle
- Hold the piping bag at a 45-degree angle, keeping consistent pressure for even shapes.
3. Wet Your Finger
- Dip your finger in water to smooth any peaks on the dough before baking.
4. Use a Template
- Draw circles or lines on parchment paper as guides for consistent sizes.
5. Space Evenly
- Leave at least 2 inches between piped shapes to allow for expansion during baking.

Troubleshooting Common Issues

1. Flat Puffs
- Cause: Oven wasn't hot enough or dough was too wet.
- Solution: Preheat the oven properly and cook the dough thoroughly on the stovetop.
2. Cracked Tops
- Cause: Uneven piping or dough was too dry.
- Solution: Ensure the dough is smooth and pipe evenly.
3. Hollow but Soggy Interior
- Cause: Underbaking.

- Solution: Bake until golden and crisp, and don't open the oven door during baking.

Conclusion

Mastering choux pastry opens the door to a world of culinary possibilities, from indulgent éclairs and cream puffs to savory gougères. By understanding the science of steam, perfecting your piping technique, and following the step-by-step recipes in this chapter, you'll gain the skills to create flawless choux pastries every time.

In the next chapter, we'll explore filo and phyllo pastries, diving into the art of working with delicate, paper-thin sheets to create exquisite sweet and savory dishes. Let's continue the journey!

Chapter 6: Tarts and Tartlets

Tarts and tartlets are quintessential sweet pastries, celebrated for their versatility, elegance, and ability to impress with both flavor and presentation. Whether it's the tang of a lemon tart, the richness of a chocolate ganache tart, or the vibrant allure of fruit tartlets, these pastries are a testament to the harmony of a perfectly baked crust and well-balanced filling.

This chapter will guide you through the techniques required to master tarts and tartlets, provide recipes for three classic variations, and offer tips for decorating them with an eye for detail and elegance.

Techniques for Blind-Baking and Filling Tarts

A successful tart begins with a well-baked crust that complements the filling. Whether you're working with a custard-based filling or a chilled ganache, the crust must provide the right balance of structure and flavor.

1. Blind-Baking: What and Why

Blind-baking is the process of pre-baking the tart shell without the filling. This technique ensures the crust remains crisp and avoids becoming soggy when filled with wet or custard-based fillings.

Steps for Blind-Baking:

1. Prepare the Dough: Roll out your tart dough (shortcrust pastry works best) to about 1/8 inch thickness and fit it into your tart pan. Trim the edges for a clean finish.

2. Chill the Shell: Refrigerate the lined tart pan for at least 30 minutes to relax the gluten and prevent shrinking during baking.

3. Line and Fill: Place a sheet of parchment paper or aluminum foil over the dough, ensuring it covers the edges. Fill with pie weights, dried beans, or rice to keep the dough from puffing up.

4. Bake: Preheat the oven to 375°F (190°C) and bake the tart shell for 15–20 minutes until the edges are set and lightly golden.

5. Remove Weights: Carefully remove the weights and parchment paper. Return the shell to the oven for another 5–10 minutes to allow the bottom to bake fully.

2. Filling the Tart

Filling a tart depends on the type of tart you're making:

- Custard or Ganache Tarts: Pour the filling into the pre-baked shell and bake again if necessary.

- Chilled Tarts: For fillings like pastry cream or ganache that set in the refrigerator, ensure the shell is completely cool before filling.

- Fruit Tarts: Spread a thin layer of jam or glaze on the base before adding fresh fruit to prevent the crust from absorbing moisture.

3. Preventing Common Issues

- Shrinking Crusts: Always chill the dough before baking and avoid stretching it when fitting it into the pan.

- Soggy Bottoms: Blind-bake the crust and brush it with a thin layer of beaten egg yolk or melted chocolate to create a moisture barrier.

- Cracks in the Shell: Patch small cracks with extra dough or a mixture of flour and water before baking.

Recipes

1. Lemon Tart

Bright and zesty, the lemon tart is a timeless dessert that balances tangy citrus with a buttery crust.

Ingredients (Serves 8):

For the Crust:
- 1 1/2 cups (190 g) all-purpose flour
- 1/2 cup (115 g) unsalted butter, chilled and cubed
- 1/4 cup (50 g) powdered sugar
- 1 large egg yolk
- 2 tablespoons ice water

For the Filling:
- 3/4 cup (180 ml) freshly squeezed lemon juice
- Zest of 2 lemons
- 1 cup (200 g) granulated sugar
- 4 large eggs
- 1/2 cup (120 ml) heavy cream

Instructions:

1. Make the Crust:
- Combine flour, butter, and powdered sugar in a bowl. Rub the butter into the flour until it resembles coarse crumbs. Add egg yolk and ice water, mixing until the dough comes together. Wrap and chill for 30 minutes.

2. Blind-Bake the Shell:
- Roll out the dough, fit it into a 9-inch tart pan, and blind-bake as described above. Let cool completely.

3. Prepare the Filling:
- In a bowl, whisk together lemon juice, zest, sugar, eggs, and heavy cream until smooth.

4. Bake the Tart:
- Pour the filling into the cooled tart shell. Bake at 325°F (165°C) for 20–25 minutes, or until the filling is just set. Let cool and refrigerate before serving.

2. Chocolate Ganache Tart

Rich and decadent, this tart is a chocolate lover's dream.

Ingredients (Serves 8):

For the Crust:
  - Same as Lemon Tart
  For the Ganache:
  - 8 ounces (225 g) semisweet chocolate, chopped
  - 1 cup (240 ml) heavy cream
  - 2 tablespoons unsalted butter, softened
  - 1 teaspoon vanilla extract

Instructions:

1. Make the Crust:
  - Follow the same steps as the Lemon Tart crust. Cool completely.
  2. Prepare the Ganache:
  - Heat the heavy cream in a saucepan until just simmering. Pour over the chopped chocolate and let sit for 2 minutes. Stir until smooth. Add butter and vanilla, mixing until glossy.
  3. Assemble the Tart:
  - Pour the ganache into the cooled crust, spreading evenly. Chill in the refrigerator for at least 2 hours before serving.
  4. Decorate:
  - Garnish with whipped cream, chocolate shavings, or berries.

3. Fruit Tartlets

These mini tarts are vibrant, colorful, and perfect for showcasing fresh seasonal fruits.

Ingredients (Makes 12):

For the Crust:
  - Same as Lemon Tart
  For the Filling:

- 2 cups pastry cream (see Chapter 9 for recipe)
For the Topping:
- Assorted fruits: berries, kiwi, mango, etc.
- 1/4 cup (60 ml) apricot jam, warmed

Instructions:

1. Make the Crusts:
- Roll out the dough and cut into 4-inch circles. Fit into a muffin tin or tartlet pans. Blind-bake as described above and let cool.
2. Assemble the Tartlets:
- Spoon pastry cream into each tartlet shell. Top with sliced fruit arranged in a decorative pattern.
3. Glaze the Fruits:
- Brush the fruit with warmed apricot jam for a glossy finish.

Decorating Tips for Elegant Presentation

1. Garnishes and Glazes
- Use powdered sugar, chocolate drizzles, or edible flowers to elevate the presentation.
- For fruit tarts, a thin layer of glaze adds shine and keeps fruit fresh.
2. Precision and Symmetry
- Arrange fruits or decorative elements in concentric circles or patterns for a polished look.
3. Adding Height
- Use whipped cream or meringue to create height and dimension on tarts.
4. Edible Accents
- Add candied citrus peel, chocolate curls, or crushed nuts for texture and flavor.

Conclusion

Tarts and tartlets are a celebration of both flavor and artistry. By mastering techniques like blind-baking, perfecting fillings, and embracing decorative flourishes, you can create stunning pastries that captivate both the eyes and the palate. Whether you're serving a classic lemon tart, a decadent chocolate ganache tart, or vibrant fruit tartlets, these recipes and techniques will help you shine in the kitchen.

In the next chapter, we'll dive into the world of *"Classic Pastries from Around the World,"* exploring the unique and beloved pastries that have become culinary icons in their respective cultures. Let's continue!

Chapter 7: Classic Pastries from Around the World

Pastries are more than just a culinary indulgence—they are cultural treasures that reflect the history, geography, and creativity of the people who make them. Each region of the world has developed its own unique pastry traditions, showcasing an incredible diversity of flavors, techniques, and ingredients.

In this chapter, we'll embark on a journey to explore the fascinating stories and intricate techniques behind three iconic global pastries: French croissants, Italian sfogliatelle, and Middle Eastern baklava. You'll also learn how to recreate these classics in your own kitchen, along with insights into the cultural significance and ingredients that make each pastry unique.

Exploring Global Pastry Traditions

Pastries have traveled across continents, adapting to local ingredients and culinary styles. Their evolution reflects centuries of trade, conquest, and cultural exchange.

1. French Pastries

France is synonymous with pastry perfection. From the buttery layers of a croissant to the delicate shells of a macaron, French pastries are renowned for their precision and elegance. Techniques like lamination (used for croissants) and the art of pâte à choux have influenced baking worldwide.

2. Italian Pastries

Italy's pastries are rooted in tradition, with recipes passed down through generations. Regional specialties abound, such as the layered sfogliatelle from Naples, cannoli from Sicily, and panettone from Milan. Italian pastries often highlight simple, high-quality ingredients like ricotta, citrus, and nuts.

3. Middle Eastern Pastries

Middle Eastern pastries are celebrated for their intricate layers and syrup-soaked sweetness. Phyllo dough, nuts, and fragrant syrups are the foundation of treats like baklava and kunafa. These pastries are often associated with hospitality and special occasions.

Recipes

Now, let's dive into three classic pastry recipes, each representing the rich tradition of its region.

1. French Croissants

Croissants are the quintessential laminated pastry, with their iconic flaky layers and buttery aroma. While making croissants from scratch requires patience, the result is a pastry that's crisp on the outside, tender on the inside, and undeniably rewarding.

Ingredients (Makes 12 croissants):

For the Dough:
- 4 cups (500 g) all-purpose flour
- 1/4 cup (50 g) granulated sugar
- 2 teaspoons salt
- 1 tablespoon instant yeast
- 1 1/4 cups (300 ml) cold milk
- 2 tablespoons unsalted butter, softened

For the Butter Block:
- 1 cup (225 g) unsalted butter, chilled but pliable

For the Egg Wash:
- 1 egg, beaten
- 1 tablespoon milk

Instructions:

1. Make the Dough:
   - In a large bowl, mix flour, sugar, salt, and yeast. Add milk and softened butter, kneading until smooth. Shape into a rectangle, wrap in plastic, and chill for 1 hour.

2. Prepare the Butter Block:

- Place the butter between two sheets of parchment paper. Pound and shape into a 5x5-inch square. Chill until firm but pliable.

3. Laminate the Dough:

- Roll the dough into a 10x20-inch rectangle. Place the butter block in the center. Fold the dough over the butter, encasing it completely. Roll out again and fold into thirds. Chill for 30 minutes. Repeat this process three times to create layers.

4. Shape the Croissants:

- Roll the dough into a 10x20-inch rectangle and cut into triangles. Roll each triangle from the base to the tip, tucking the tip underneath to secure.

5. Proof and Bake:

- Place croissants on a baking sheet and proof at room temperature until doubled in size (about 2 hours). Brush with egg wash. Bake at 375°F (190°C) for 15–20 minutes until golden brown.

2. Italian Sfogliatelle

Sfogliatelle, also known as "lobster tails," are a traditional Neapolitan pastry featuring thin, crisp layers filled with sweetened ricotta. Their intricate folds and delicate crunch make them a showstopper.

Ingredients (Makes 12):

For the Dough:
- 3 cups (375 g) all-purpose flour
- 1/4 teaspoon salt
- 1/2 cup (120 ml) water
- 1/4 cup (60 ml) lard or butter, melted
For the Filling:
- 1 cup (250 g) ricotta cheese, drained
- 1/2 cup (100 g) granulated sugar
- 1/2 teaspoon cinnamon
- Zest of 1 lemon
- 1/4 cup (50 g) semolina flour, cooked and cooled
For Brushing:

- 1/2 cup (120 g) melted butter

Instructions:

1. Make the Dough:
- Combine flour, salt, and water in a bowl. Knead into a smooth dough, wrap in plastic, and let rest for 1 hour.
2. Prepare the Filling:
- Mix ricotta, sugar, cinnamon, lemon zest, and cooked semolina until smooth. Chill until needed.
3. Roll and Layer:
- Roll the dough into a paper-thin sheet. Brush with melted butter, then roll tightly into a log. Slice the log into 1/2-inch rounds.
4. Shape the Pastries:
- Flatten each round with your fingers to create a shell shape. Fill with ricotta mixture and pinch the edges to seal.
5. Bake:
- Place on a baking sheet and bake at 375°F (190°C) for 20–25 minutes until golden and crisp.

3. Middle Eastern Baklava

Baklava is a rich, syrup-soaked pastry made with layers of phyllo dough, chopped nuts, and a fragrant honey syrup. This dessert is a staple in Middle Eastern and Mediterranean cuisines.

Ingredients (Serves 12):

For the Pastry:
- 1 package phyllo dough (16 oz/450 g), thawed
- 1 cup (225 g) unsalted butter, melted
- 2 cups (250 g) chopped walnuts or pistachios
For the Syrup:
- 1 cup (240 ml) water
- 1 cup (200 g) sugar

- 1/2 cup (120 ml) honey
- 1 teaspoon rosewater or orange blossom water (optional)

Instructions:

1. Prepare the Syrup:
- Combine water, sugar, and honey in a saucepan. Simmer for 10 minutes, then stir in rosewater. Cool completely.
2. Assemble the Baklava:
- Brush a 9x13-inch pan with melted butter. Layer 8 sheets of phyllo, brushing each with butter. Sprinkle a thin layer of nuts. Repeat until all ingredients are used, finishing with 8 layers of phyllo.
3. Cut and Bake:
- Use a sharp knife to cut the pastry into diamonds or squares. Bake at 350°F (175°C) for 40–50 minutes until golden and crisp.
4. Add Syrup:
- Pour cooled syrup over the hot baklava. Let soak for several hours before serving.

Understanding Cultural Differences in Techniques and Ingredients

Each pastry reflects the ingredients and culinary practices of its origin:
- French Croissants: Highlight precise lamination techniques and rely on butter for their rich flavor.
- Italian Sfogliatelle: Use lard or butter for crisp layers and feature fillings like ricotta, citrus, and semolina.
- Middle Eastern Baklava: Emphasize sweetness and fragrance, with ingredients like rosewater, honey, and nuts.

Conclusion

Classic pastries like croissants, sfogliatelle, and baklava demonstrate the diversity and richness of global pastry traditions. By understanding their cultural origins and mastering their techniques, you can bring the world of pastry to your kitchen. These recipes not only delight the palate but also serve as a connection to the rich culinary histories they represent.

In the next chapter, we'll dive into *Danish Pastries and Other Laminated Treats,* exploring the magic of yeast-raised pastries and their delectable fillings. Let's continue this delicious journey!

Chapter 8: Danish Pastries and Other Laminated Treats

Danish pastries and other laminated yeast-based treats are a delightful fusion of buttery richness, tender layers, and sweet or savory fillings. These pastries, known for their intricate textures and irresistible flavors, are a testament to the art of lamination combined with the science of yeast fermentation.

In this chapter, we will delve into the process of creating laminated yeast dough, a foundational skill for crafting iconic pastries like cinnamon rolls, classic Danish pastries, and kouign-amann. We will explore the techniques needed to balance the buttery richness of the dough with a variety of fillings and toppings, ensuring every bite is a perfect harmony of flavor and texture.

Understanding Laminated Yeast Dough

Laminated yeast dough combines the characteristics of traditional yeast dough with the layering techniques of puff pastry. The result is a pastry that is light, tender, and slightly chewy, with a rich buttery flavor.

1. The Role of Yeast in Laminated Dough

- Leavening Power: Yeast ferments the dough, creating carbon dioxide that makes the pastry rise and gives it a tender, airy crumb.
   - Flavor Development: Fermentation contributes a subtle tang and depth of flavor to the dough.
   - Structure: The gluten in the dough provides elasticity, allowing it to stretch and encase the butter layers during lamination.

2. The Importance of Butter in Laminated Dough

Butter is the cornerstone of laminated dough, responsible for the flaky layers and rich flavor.

- Plasticity: Butter must be pliable but not too soft, ensuring it can be rolled into thin layers without breaking or melting.

- Flavor: High-quality butter, preferably European-style with higher fat content, enhances the pastry's flavor.

3. The Lamination Process

Laminating yeast dough involves folding and rolling butter into the dough to create layers. These layers puff up during baking as the water in the butter turns to steam, separating the dough and creating a flaky texture.

Step-by-Step Guide to Laminated Yeast Dough

Ingredients (Makes Enough for 12 Pastries):

- 4 cups (500 g) all-purpose flour
    - 1/4 cup (50 g) granulated sugar
    - 2 teaspoons salt
    - 1 tablespoon instant yeast
    - 1 cup (240 ml) whole milk, warmed
    - 1/4 cup (60 g) unsalted butter, softened
    - 1 large egg
    - 1 cup (225 g) unsalted butter, chilled and shaped into a square

Instructions:

Step 1: Make the Dough

1. In a large bowl, combine flour, sugar, salt, and yeast.

2. Add the warm milk, softened butter, and egg. Mix until a shaggy dough forms.

3. Knead the dough on a lightly floured surface for 8–10 minutes until smooth and elastic.

4. Shape the dough into a rectangle, wrap in plastic, and chill in the refrigerator for 1 hour.

Step 2: Prepare the Butter Block

1. Place the chilled butter between two sheets of parchment paper.

2. Pound and shape the butter into a 5x5-inch square. Refrigerate until firm but pliable.

Step 3: Encasing the Butter

1. Roll the dough into a 10x10-inch square. Place the butter block diagonally in the center of the dough.

2. Fold the corners of the dough over the butter, encasing it completely. Pinch the seams to seal.

Step 4: Laminate the Dough

1. Roll the dough into a 10x20-inch rectangle.

2. Perform a *single fold:* Fold the top third of the dough down and the bottom third up, like folding a letter. Rotate 90 degrees.

3. Chill the dough for 30 minutes. Repeat this rolling and folding process two more times, chilling the dough between each fold.

Step 5: Final Chill

Wrap the laminated dough in plastic wrap and refrigerate for at least 2 hours or overnight before shaping.

Recipes

1. Classic Danish Pastries

Danish pastries are characterized by their light, flaky dough and sweet fillings. These versatile treats can be filled with fruit, custard, or cream cheese.

Ingredients (Makes 12):

For the Filling:
- 1 cup (250 g) cream cheese, softened
- 1/4 cup (50 g) granulated sugar
- 1 teaspoon vanilla extract
For the Glaze:
- 1/2 cup (60 g) powdered sugar

- 1 tablespoon milk

Instructions:

1. Shape the Dough: Roll the laminated dough into a 12x16-inch rectangle. Cut into 4-inch squares.

2. Fill and Fold: Spoon 1 tablespoon of filling onto the center of each square. Fold the corners over the filling, pressing lightly to seal.

3. Proof and Bake: Place on a baking sheet, cover, and proof at room temperature for 1–2 hours until puffy. Bake at 375°F (190°C) for 15–20 minutes until golden.

4. Glaze: Mix powdered sugar and milk to form a glaze. Drizzle over the cooled pastries.

2. Cinnamon Rolls

Soft and gooey, cinnamon rolls are a crowd-pleasing pastry perfect for breakfast or dessert.

Ingredients (Makes 12):

For the Filling:
- 1/2 cup (100 g) brown sugar
- 2 teaspoons cinnamon
- 1/4 cup (60 g) unsalted butter, softened
For the Frosting:
- 1/2 cup (115 g) cream cheese, softened
- 1 cup (125 g) powdered sugar
- 1 teaspoon vanilla extract

Instructions:

1. Shape the Dough: Roll the laminated dough into a 10x18-inch rectangle.

2. Spread the Filling: Mix brown sugar and cinnamon. Spread softened butter over the dough and sprinkle with the sugar mixture.

3. Roll and Slice: Roll the dough tightly from the long side. Cut into 12 equal slices.

4. Proof and Bake: Arrange in a greased baking dish. Proof at room temperature for 1–2 hours. Bake at 375°F (190°C) for 20–25 minutes.

5. Frost: Mix cream cheese, powdered sugar, and vanilla until smooth. Spread over warm rolls.

3. Kouign-Amann

A specialty from Brittany, France, kouign-amann combines caramelized sugar with buttery layers for a rich, decadent treat.

Ingredients (Makes 12):

For the Sugar Layer:
- 1/2 cup (100 g) granulated sugar

Instructions:

1. Shape the Dough: Roll the laminated dough into a 12x12-inch square. Sprinkle evenly with sugar.

2. Fold and Roll: Fold the dough into thirds, then roll into a rectangle. Repeat twice more, chilling the dough if it becomes too soft.

3. Cut and Shape: Roll the dough into a 12x16-inch rectangle and cut into 12 squares. Fold the corners of each square into the center, creating a pinwheel shape.

4. Proof and Bake: Place in greased muffin tins. Proof for 1 hour. Bake at 400°F (200°C) for 25–30 minutes until golden and caramelized.

Balancing Buttery Richness with Sweet Fillings

The key to a perfect laminated pastry is balance. The dough should complement, not overpower, the filling.

- Light Fillings: Use fruit or cream cheese to balance the richness of the dough.

- Bold Flavors: Add spices, citrus zest, or extracts to fillings for contrast.

- Sweet Toppings: Glazes, powdered sugar, or caramelized sugar enhance the pastry without making it cloyingly sweet.

Conclusion

Danish pastries, cinnamon rolls, and kouign-amann represent the pinnacle of laminated yeast dough artistry. By mastering the techniques of lamination, shaping, and filling, you can create pastries that are not only visually stunning but also deeply satisfying to eat. These treats are perfect for any occasion, offering endless opportunities for creativity and indulgence.

In the next chapter, we'll explore *"Tarts and Tartlets,"* diving into the art of blind-baking and filling to craft exquisite pastry creations. Let's keep rolling!

Chapter 9: Pastry Creams and Fillings

The heart of any exceptional pastry lies in its filling. Whether it's the luscious vanilla pastry cream in an éclair, the airy richness of chocolate mousse in a tart, or the tangy brightness of a fruit curd in a layered dessert, fillings elevate pastries to indulgent treats. Mastering these components requires understanding the delicate balance of flavor, texture, and consistency.

In this chapter, we will explore essential recipes for vanilla pastry cream, chocolate mousse, and fruit curds. You'll learn techniques for filling pastries like éclairs and tarts, along with tips for flavoring and thickening to ensure your creams and fillings are always a success.

The Essentials of Pastry Creams and Fillings

Pastry creams and fillings are as diverse as the pastries they enhance. Each type has unique characteristics, but they all share the common goal of providing flavor, moisture, and textural contrast.

1. Key Components of Pastry Fillings

- Flavor: Use high-quality ingredients like pure vanilla extract, fresh fruit, and premium chocolate to ensure the best taste.

- Texture: A filling's texture should complement the pastry. For instance, a silky cream pairs well with a crisp shell, while a rich mousse works beautifully in soft, tender tarts.

- Stability: Proper thickening agents, like cornstarch or gelatin, ensure the filling holds its shape without becoming rubbery or overly stiff.

2. Techniques for Success

- Control Temperature: Many fillings require precise heating to thicken without curdling or separating.

- Avoid Overmixing: Overworking creams or mousses can lead to a loss of structure and airiness.

- Chill Properly: Allow fillings to cool and set before using, as this improves both flavor and consistency.

Recipes

1. Vanilla Pastry Cream

Vanilla pastry cream, or crème pâtissière, is a classic filling for éclairs, tarts, and mille-feuille. Its rich, custard-like texture and sweet, aromatic flavor make it a versatile choice.

Ingredients (Makes 2 cups):

- 2 cups (500 ml) whole milk
    - 1/2 cup (100 g) granulated sugar
    - 1/4 cup (30 g) cornstarch
    - 4 large egg yolks
    - 1 teaspoon pure vanilla extract
    - 2 tablespoons unsalted butter

Instructions:

1. Heat the Milk:
    - In a saucepan, heat milk over medium heat until it begins to steam. Remove from heat.
    2. Whisk the Egg Mixture:
    - In a bowl, whisk together sugar, cornstarch, and egg yolks until smooth and pale.
    3. Temper the Eggs:
    - Gradually add the hot milk to the egg mixture, whisking constantly to prevent curdling.

4. Cook the Cream:

- Return the mixture to the saucepan and cook over medium heat, whisking constantly, until thickened and bubbling.

5. Add Butter and Vanilla:

- Remove from heat and stir in butter and vanilla. Strain through a fine-mesh sieve for a silky texture.

6. Chill:

- Cover with plastic wrap pressed directly onto the surface to prevent a skin from forming. Chill completely before using.

2. Chocolate Mousse

Chocolate mousse is a decadent filling that's light yet indulgent. Perfect for tarts, layered pastries, or served on its own.

Ingredients (Serves 6):

- 6 ounces (170 g) bittersweet chocolate, chopped
  - 3 large eggs, separated
  - 1/4 cup (50 g) granulated sugar
  - 1 cup (240 ml) heavy cream

Instructions:

1. Melt the Chocolate:

- Place chocolate in a heatproof bowl over a simmering pot of water. Stir until melted and smooth. Let cool slightly.

2. Beat the Egg Yolks:

- Whisk the yolks with 2 tablespoons of sugar until pale and thick. Stir into the melted chocolate.

3. Whip the Egg Whites:

- In a clean bowl, beat egg whites with the remaining sugar until stiff peaks form. Gently fold into the chocolate mixture.

4. Whip the Cream:

- Beat the heavy cream until soft peaks form. Fold into the chocolate mixture.

5. Chill:

- Spoon or pipe the mousse into a tart shell or serving dish. Refrigerate for at least 2 hours before serving.

3. Fruit Curd

Bright and tangy, fruit curds are an excellent filling for tarts, cakes, and pastries. Lemon curd is the most popular, but you can experiment with other fruits like lime, passion fruit, or raspberry.

Ingredients (Makes 1 cup):

- 1/2 cup (120 ml) freshly squeezed lemon juice
    - Zest of 1 lemon
    - 1/2 cup (100 g) granulated sugar
    - 3 large eggs
    - 6 tablespoons (85 g) unsalted butter, cubed

Instructions:

1. Combine Ingredients:
    - In a heatproof bowl, whisk together lemon juice, zest, sugar, and eggs.
    2. Cook Over a Double Boiler:
    - Place the bowl over simmering water, whisking constantly, until the mixture thickens and coats the back of a spoon.
    3. Add Butter:
    - Remove from heat and whisk in the butter until smooth.
    4. Strain and Chill:
    - Strain the curd to remove zest and any cooked egg bits. Cover with plastic wrap and chill.

Techniques for Filling Pastries

1. Filling Éclairs

- Use a skewer to poke a small hole in the end of each éclair.

- Fit a piping bag with a small round tip, fill it with pastry cream, and pipe into the éclair until full.

2. Filling Tarts

- Spoon or pipe the filling into a pre-baked tart shell.

- Smooth the top with an offset spatula for a polished finish.

3. Filling Layered Pastries

- Use a piping bag for precision when adding fillings between pastry layers.

- Alternate layers of mousse or pastry cream with sponge cake or puff pastry for a stunning presentation.

Tips for Flavoring and Thickening Creams

1. Flavoring Techniques

- Extracts: Add vanilla, almond, or coffee extract for a subtle yet distinct flavor.

- Spices: Incorporate cinnamon, nutmeg, or cardamom for warmth.

- Citrus: Use zest or juice to brighten flavors.

- Infusions: Steep herbs or spices in warm milk before making pastry cream.

2. Thickening Agents

- Cornstarch: Creates a smooth, stable consistency in pastry cream.

- Gelatin: Adds structure to mousses and chilled fillings.

- Agar-Agar: A vegetarian alternative to gelatin.

3. Avoid Over-Thickening

- Gradually add thickeners, as overuse can result in a rubbery texture.

- Test consistency by cooling a small sample before adjusting further.

Conclusion

Pastry creams tend fillings are the foundation of countless desserts, from éclairs and tarts to layered cakes and pastries. By mastering classic recipes like vanilla pastry cream, chocolate mousse, and fruit curds, you'll unlock endless possibilities for creating indulgent treats. With the techniques and tips provided, you can ensure your fillings are always flavorful, perfectly textured, and a joy to work with.

In the next chapter, we'll explore the art of *"Decorating Pastries,"* delving into the tools, techniques, and creativity needed to make your pastries as visually stunning as they are delicious. Let's continue!

Chapter 10: Pies, Pasties, and Hand Pies

Savory pastries such as pies, pasties, and hand pies have been beloved comfort foods for centuries. These versatile pastries combine a flaky, buttery crust with hearty, flavorful fillings, making them perfect for meals, snacks, or special occasions. From the creamy chicken pot pie to the rustic vegetable pasty and the indulgent cheese-filled hand pie, each variation offers unique textures and tastes.

In this chapter, we'll explore the craft of savory pastry doughs, provide detailed recipes for three iconic savory pastries, and discuss techniques for layering flavors in fillings to achieve depth and balance.

Crafting Savory Pastry Doughs

The foundation of any great savory pastry lies in its crust. While similar to sweet pastry doughs, savory doughs often incorporate additional ingredients like herbs, cheese, or spices to complement the fillings.

1. The Essentials of Savory Dough

Savory pastry dough must strike a balance between flakiness and structure, ensuring it can hold hearty fillings without becoming soggy.

Key Characteristics:

- Tender Flakiness: Achieved by layering cold fat (butter, lard, or shortening) with flour.
    - Structural Integrity: Enough gluten development to prevent crumbling.
    - Flavorful Enhancements: Herbs, spices, or grated cheese can be added for extra flavor.

2. Tips for Perfect Savory Dough

- Keep Ingredients Cold: Cold butter and water are essential for maintaining flakiness.

- Use Minimal Water: Add just enough water to bring the dough together without overhydrating.

- Chill Before Rolling: Refrigerate the dough for at least 30 minutes to relax the gluten and firm up the fat.

- Blind Bake When Necessary: Pre-baking the crust prevents sogginess when using wetter fillings.

3. Basic Savory Pastry Dough Recipe

Ingredients:

- 2 1/2 cups (315 g) all-purpose flour
    - 1 teaspoon salt
    - 1 teaspoon dried herbs (e.g., thyme or rosemary)
    - 1 cup (225 g) unsalted butter, chilled and cubed
    - 1/4–1/2 cup (60–120 ml) ice water

Instructions:

1. Mix Dry Ingredients:
    - In a large bowl, whisk together flour, salt, and dried herbs.
    2. Incorporate Butter:
    - Add the chilled butter to the flour mixture. Use a pastry cutter or your fingertips to work the butter into the flour until it resembles coarse crumbs.
    3. Add Water Gradually:
    - Sprinkle in ice water, 1 tablespoon at a time, mixing gently until the dough just comes together.
    4. Chill the Dough:
    - Shape the dough into a disc, wrap it in plastic wrap, and refrigerate for at least 30 minutes.

Recipes

1. Chicken Pot Pie

A creamy, hearty chicken pot pie is a classic comfort food. Its flaky crust pairs perfectly with a rich filling of chicken and vegetables in a velvety sauce.

Ingredients (Serves 4):

For the Filling:
- 2 tablespoons unsalted butter
- 1 small onion, diced
- 2 medium carrots, diced
- 1 cup (150 g) frozen peas
- 2 cups (500 ml) chicken stock
- 1/2 cup (120 ml) heavy cream
- 3 cups (450 g) cooked chicken, shredded
- 1/4 cup (30 g) all-purpose flour
- 1 teaspoon dried thyme
- Salt and pepper to taste
For the Crust:
- 1 recipe basic savory pastry dough

Instructions:

1. Prepare the Filling:

- In a large skillet, melt butter over medium heat. Add onion and carrots, cooking until softened.

- Sprinkle flour over the vegetables and stir for 1–2 minutes. Gradually add chicken stock, whisking until smooth.

- Stir in heavy cream, thyme, chicken, and peas. Season with salt and pepper. Simmer until thickened.

2. Assemble the Pie:

- Preheat the oven to 375°F (190°C). Roll out the pastry dough and fit it into a pie dish. Pour in the filling.

- Roll out a second sheet of dough for the top crust. Place it over the filling, crimping the edges to seal. Cut small slits in the top to allow steam to escape.

3. Bake:

- Brush the crust with an egg wash (1 beaten egg mixed with 1 tablespoon water). Bake for 35–40 minutes, or until golden brown. Let cool slightly before serving.

2. Vegetable Pasties

Originating from Cornwall, England, pasties are rustic hand pies traditionally filled with meat and vegetables. This vegetable version is hearty and satisfying, making it a great vegetarian option.

Ingredients (Makes 6 Pasties):

For the Filling:
   - 2 medium potatoes, diced
   - 1 medium turnip, diced
   - 1 medium carrot, diced
   - 1/2 cup (75 g) frozen peas
   - 1 small onion, diced
   - 1 teaspoon dried rosemary
   - Salt and pepper to taste
   For the Dough:
   - 1 recipe basic savory pastry dough

Instructions:

1. Prepare the Filling:
   - Combine diced vegetables, rosemary, salt, and pepper in a bowl.
   2. Assemble the Pasties:
   - Preheat the oven to 375°F (190°C). Roll out the dough and cut into 6-inch circles.
   - Place 1/2 cup of filling on one side of each circle. Fold the dough over and crimp the edges to seal.
   3. Bake:

- Place pasties on a baking sheet and brush with egg wash. Bake for 30–35 minutes, or until golden brown.

3. Cheese Hand Pies

Cheese hand pies are simple yet indulgent. Their gooey filling and buttery crust make them a favorite for all ages.

Ingredients (Makes 8):

For the Filling:
- 1 cup (100 g) shredded cheddar cheese
- 1/2 cup (50 g) grated Parmesan cheese
- 1 teaspoon Dijon mustard
For the Dough:
- 1 recipe basic savory pastry dough

Instructions:

1. Prepare the Filling:
- In a bowl, mix cheddar, Parmesan, and Dijon mustard.
2. Assemble the Hand Pies:
- Preheat the oven to 375°F (190°C). Roll out the dough and cut into 4-inch squares.
- Spoon 1 tablespoon of filling onto each square. Fold over into a triangle and crimp the edges to seal.
3. Bake:
- Place hand pies on a baking sheet and brush with egg wash. Bake for 20–25 minutes, or until golden brown.

Layering Flavors in Savory Fillings

The key to a standout savory pastry is a filling that balances rich, bold flavors with complementary textures. Here's how to achieve that:
1. Build a Flavor Base

- Start with aromatics like onions, garlic, and leeks sautéed in butter or oil.
2. Add Depth
- Use herbs, spices, or umami-rich ingredients like mushrooms, cheese, or miso to enhance complexity.
3. Balance Richness
- Incorporate fresh elements like vegetables, citrus zest, or a splash of vinegar to cut through heavier flavors.
4. Choose the Right Texture
- Combine soft, creamy elements (e.g., mashed potatoes or cheese) with firmer ingredients (e.g., diced vegetables or meat) for textural contrast.

Conclusion

Pies, pasties, and hand pies are timeless savory pastries that deliver comfort and flavor in every bite. By mastering the craft of savory pastry doughs, experimenting with classic recipes like chicken pot pie, vegetable pasties, and cheese hand pies, and learning to layer flavors effectively, you'll be able to create satisfying and versatile dishes.

In the next chapter, we'll explore the art of *"Savory Tarts and Quiches,"* diving into the techniques for crafting elegant and flavorful pastry dishes perfect for any occasion. Let's continue!

Chapter 11: Quiches and Savory Tarts

Quiches and savory tarts are the epitome of elegant comfort food, combining flaky, buttery crusts with rich, flavorful fillings. Whether you're crafting a classic Quiche Lorraine, a vibrant roasted vegetable tart, or delicate goat cheese tartlets, the key to success lies in mastering the balance between a well-baked crust and a perfectly set custard or filling.

This chapter will guide you through the techniques for creating quiches and savory tarts, provide detailed recipes for three timeless variations, and share tips for pre-baking crusts to ensure they remain crisp and delicious.

The Anatomy of a Perfect Quiche or Tart

Quiches and savory tarts share similar components, but each has unique characteristics that define its flavor and texture.

1. The Crust
The crust serves as the foundation for both quiches and tarts, providing structure and a contrasting texture to the creamy filling.
- Shortcrust Pastry: A classic choice for quiches, offering a tender, buttery base.
- Puff Pastry: Used for lighter, flakier tarts.
- Savory Additions: Incorporate herbs, cheese, or spices into the dough for added flavor.
2. The Filling
The filling is the star of the dish, with endless possibilities for customization.
- Custard Base: Quiches rely on a mixture of eggs and dairy (cream, milk, or a combination) for a silky, rich texture.
- Vegetables and Proteins: Ingredients like roasted vegetables, cheese, bacon, or seafood can add depth and complexity.
- Flavor Enhancers: Herbs, spices, and aromatics elevate the overall profile.
3. The Balance

Achieving the right balance between crust, custard, and filling is crucial.

- Crust Thickness: Too thick, and it overwhelms the filling; too thin, and it may collapse.

- Custard Ratio: The egg-to-dairy ratio affects texture. A general guideline is 1 egg per 1/2 cup of dairy.

- Filling Distribution: Evenly distribute fillings to ensure a harmonious bite every time.

Tips for Pre-Baking Crusts

Pre-baking, or blind baking, ensures the crust remains crisp, even with wet fillings.

1. Why Pre-Bake?

- Prevents sogginess by partially cooking the crust before adding the filling.

- Helps maintain the crust's structure, avoiding shrinking or puffing.

2. How to Pre-Bake:

1. Prepare the Dough: Roll out the dough and fit it into a tart pan. Trim excess dough and chill for at least 30 minutes to relax the gluten.

2. Line and Weigh: Place parchment paper or aluminum foil over the crust and fill with pie weights, dried beans, or rice.

3. Bake: Preheat the oven to 375°F (190°C). Bake the crust for 15–20 minutes until the edges are set.

4. Remove Weights: Carefully remove the parchment and weights. Bake for an additional 5–10 minutes to ensure the bottom is fully cooked.

5. Cool: Let the crust cool slightly before adding the filling.

Recipes

1. Quiche Lorraine

Quiche Lorraine is a timeless French classic, featuring a flaky crust, a creamy custard, and smoky bacon lardons.

Ingredients (Serves 6–8):

For the Crust:
- 1 1/2 cups (190 g) all-purpose flour
- 1/2 teaspoon salt
- 1/2 cup (115 g) unsalted butter, chilled and cubed
- 3–4 tablespoons ice water

For the Filling:
- 6 slices bacon, chopped
- 1 medium onion, diced
- 3 large eggs
- 1 cup (240 ml) heavy cream
- 1/2 cup (120 ml) whole milk
- 1/2 teaspoon ground nutmeg
- Salt and pepper to taste
- 1 cup (100 g) shredded Gruyère cheese

Instructions:

1. Make the Crust:

- Combine flour and salt in a bowl. Cut in the butter until the mixture resembles coarse crumbs. Add ice water, 1 tablespoon at a time, until the dough comes together. Chill for 30 minutes.

2. Pre-Bake the Crust:

- Roll out the dough, fit it into a tart pan, and blind bake as described earlier.

3. Prepare the Filling:

- Cook bacon in a skillet until crisp. Remove and drain on paper towels. In the same skillet, sauté onions until soft.

4. Mix the Custard:

- Whisk together eggs, cream, milk, nutmeg, salt, and pepper.

5. Assemble and Bake:

- Sprinkle bacon, onions, and cheese evenly over the crust. Pour the custard over the filling. Bake at 375°F (190°C) for 30–35 minutes, or until the center is set. Cool slightly before slicing.

2. Roasted Vegetable Tart

This vibrant tart showcases the natural sweetness of roasted vegetables, paired with a flaky crust and creamy filling.

Ingredients (Serves 6):

For the Crust:

- Same as Quiche Lorraine

For the Filling:

- 1 red bell pepper, sliced
- 1 zucchini, sliced
- 1 yellow squash, sliced
- 1 small eggplant, cubed
- 2 tablespoons olive oil
- Salt and pepper to taste
- 3 large eggs
- 1 cup (240 ml) heavy cream
- 1/2 cup (50 g) grated Parmesan cheese

Instructions:

1. Prepare the Vegetables:

- Toss vegetables with olive oil, salt, and pepper. Roast at 400°F (200°C) for 20 minutes, or until tender.

2. Make the Crust:
- Follow the same steps as for Quiche Lorraine.
3. Mix the Custard:
- Whisk together eggs, cream, Parmesan, salt, and pepper.
4. Assemble and Bake:
- Arrange roasted vegetables in the crust. Pour custard over the top. Bake at 375°F (190°C) for 30–35 minutes. Cool slightly before serving.

3. Goat Cheese Tartlets

These individual tartlets are elegant and packed with tangy goat cheese, making them perfect for appetizers or light meals.

Ingredients (Makes 8 Tartlets):

For the Crust:
- 1 recipe savory pastry dough
For the Filling:
- 6 ounces (170 g) goat cheese, softened
- 1/2 cup (120 ml) heavy cream
- 2 large eggs
- 1 tablespoon fresh thyme leaves
- Salt and pepper to taste

Instructions:

1. Prepare the Tartlet Shells:
- Roll out the dough and cut into 4-inch circles. Fit into tartlet pans and blind bake as described earlier.
2. Mix the Filling:
- Combine goat cheese, cream, eggs, thyme, salt, and pepper in a bowl, whisking until smooth.
3. Assemble and Bake:
- Divide the filling among the tartlet shells. Bake at 375°F (190°C) for 20–25 minutes, or until set.

Balancing Custards and Crusts

1. Custard Ratios

    - For a creamier quiche, use more cream than milk.

    - For a lighter texture, increase the milk ratio.

    2. Enhancing Crust Flavor

    - Add grated cheese, fresh herbs, or spices to the dough for extra flavor.

    3. Layering Fillings

    - Distribute heavier ingredients evenly before pouring the custard to ensure even cooking.

Conclusion

Quiches and savory tarts are versatile dishes that can be adapted to suit any occasion or flavor preference. By mastering the art of balancing crusts and custards, experimenting with a variety of fillings, and perfecting your pre-baking technique, you'll be able to create stunning and delicious pastries every time.

In the next chapter, we'll delve into the world of *"Savory Galettes and Crostatas,"* exploring their rustic charm and endless filling possibilities. Let's continue the journey!

Chapter 12: Puff Pastry Appetizers

Puff pastry, with its delicate, buttery layers and versatility, is a star ingredient in savory appetizers. From bite-sized hors d'oeuvres to elegant finger foods, puff pastry adds a touch of sophistication to any occasion. Whether you're hosting a casual get-together or an upscale soirée, puff pastry appetizers are sure to impress.

This chapter explores the creative potential of puff pastry in savory dishes, provides detailed recipes for crowd-pleasers like sausage rolls, cheese straws, and spinach puffs, and offers presentation tips to elevate your appetizers for parties and events.

The Magic of Puff Pastry

Puff pastry's light, flaky texture comes from the lamination process, which creates hundreds of thin layers of butter and dough. During baking, the water in the butter turns to steam, causing the layers to puff and crisp. This unique structure makes puff pastry the perfect base for a wide range of appetizers.

Why Puff Pastry Works for Appetizers

- Versatility: Puff pastry pairs beautifully with a variety of fillings, from creamy cheeses to savory meats and vegetables.

- Ease of Use: Pre-made puff pastry sheets are a convenient option for creating impressive appetizers without extensive preparation.

- Visual Appeal: The golden, flaky crust adds a touch of elegance to even the simplest recipes.

Tips for Working with Puff Pastry

1. Keep It Cold: Puff pastry is easiest to work with when chilled. Thaw it in the refrigerator and keep it cold while shaping.

2. Don't Overfill: Overloading puff pastry can cause it to tear or prevent proper puffing. Use a moderate amount of filling.

3. Seal Edges Well: For filled appetizers, seal edges with beaten egg to prevent leakage during baking.

4. Ventilation: Cut small slits in the pastry to allow steam to escape, ensuring even puffing.

5. Use Egg Wash: Brushing the pastry with egg wash creates a shiny, golden crust.

Recipes

1. Sausage Rolls

A classic party favorite, sausage rolls combine flaky puff pastry with a savory sausage filling. These bite-sized delights are perfect for any gathering.

Ingredients (Makes 16 Rolls):

- 1 sheet puff pastry, thawed
    - 1 pound (450 g) ground sausage (pork, chicken, or turkey)
    - 1/4 cup (30 g) breadcrumbs
    - 1 teaspoon dried sage
    - 1 teaspoon dried thyme
    - 1/4 teaspoon black pepper
    - 1 egg, beaten (for egg wash)

Instructions:

1. Prepare the Filling:
    - In a bowl, mix ground sausage, breadcrumbs, sage, thyme, and pepper until well combined.
    2. Assemble the Rolls:
    - Preheat the oven to 400°F (200°C). Roll out the puff pastry sheet on a lightly floured surface. Cut into two equal rectangles.

- Divide the sausage mixture into two portions and shape each into a log. Place one log along the edge of each pastry rectangle.

3. Roll and Seal:

- Roll the pastry tightly around the sausage, sealing the edge with beaten egg.

4. Cut and Bake:

- Slice each log into 8 pieces and place them seam-side down on a baking sheet lined with parchment paper. Brush with egg wash.

- Bake for 20–25 minutes, or until golden and cooked through.

2. Cheese Straws

Cheese straws are an easy, flavorful appetizer made by twisting puff pastry with sharp cheese and seasonings. They're crunchy, cheesy, and irresistibly good.

Ingredients (Makes 12 Straws):

- 1 sheet puff pastry, thawed
    - 1/2 cup (50 g) grated sharp cheddar cheese
    - 1/4 cup (25 g) grated Parmesan cheese
    - 1 teaspoon smoked paprika
    - 1/4 teaspoon cayenne pepper (optional)
    - 1 egg, beaten (for egg wash)

Instructions:

1. Prepare the Pastry:

- Preheat the oven to 375°F (190°C). Roll out the puff pastry sheet on a lightly floured surface.

2. Add the Cheese:

- Brush the pastry with egg wash. Sprinkle evenly with cheddar, Parmesan, paprika, and cayenne.

3. Shape the Straws:

- Fold the pastry in half to encase the cheese. Roll lightly to press the layers together. Cut into 1/2-inch strips.

- Twist each strip and place on a parchment-lined baking sheet.
4. Bake:
- Bake for 15–18 minutes, or until golden and crisp. Cool slightly before serving.

3. Spinach Puffs

Spinach puffs are flaky, buttery pastries filled with a creamy mixture of spinach, cheese, and garlic. They're perfect for vegetarians and meat lovers alike.

Ingredients (Makes 12 Puffs):

- 1 sheet puff pastry, thawed
    - 1 cup (150 g) frozen spinach, thawed and drained
    - 1/2 cup (120 g) ricotta cheese
    - 1/4 cup (30 g) grated Parmesan cheese
    - 1 clove garlic, minced
    - 1/4 teaspoon nutmeg
    - Salt and pepper to taste
    - 1 egg, beaten (for egg wash)

Instructions:

1. Prepare the Filling:
    - In a bowl, mix spinach, ricotta, Parmesan, garlic, nutmeg, salt, and pepper.
    2. Assemble the Puffs:
    - Preheat the oven to 375°F (190°C). Roll out the puff pastry sheet on a lightly floured surface and cut into 12 squares.
    - Place a spoonful of filling in the center of each square. Fold the corners over the filling to form a pouch.
    3. Seal and Bake:
    - Place the puffs on a parchment-lined baking sheet and brush with egg wash.
    - Bake for 20–25 minutes, or until golden and puffed.

Presentation Ideas for Parties and Events

Elegant presentation can elevate puff pastry appetizers from simple snacks to stunning showpieces. Here are some tips to impress your guests:

1. Use Serving Platters
    - Arrange appetizers on tiered platters or wooden boards for visual interest.
    - Group similar items together for a clean, organized look.
    2. Garnish Thoughtfully
    - Add fresh herbs like parsley or thyme to complement the flavors.
    - Sprinkle appetizers with sesame seeds, poppy seeds, or grated cheese before baking for added texture and flair.
    3. Create Mini Versions
    - Make bite-sized versions of appetizers for easier handling at parties.
    4. Label Your Creations
    - Use small cards or chalkboard signs to label each appetizer, especially if they include allergens like nuts or dairy.
    5. Pair with Dips
    - Serve puff pastry appetizers with complementary dips or sauces, such as honey mustard, marinara, or garlic aioli.

Conclusion

Puff pastry appetizers like sausage rolls, cheese straws, and spinach puffs are versatile, delicious, and always a hit at gatherings. By mastering the techniques for working with puff pastry and experimenting with creative fillings and flavors, you can create appetizers that are as visually appealing as they are satisfying. Whether served at an intimate dinner or a grand event, these appetizers are guaranteed to leave a lasting impression.

In the next chapter, we'll explore the art of *"Layered Desserts with Puff Pastry,"* diving into sweet creations that showcase the pastry's versatility and elegance. Let's continue crafting culinary magic!

Chapter 13: Filo and Phyllo Pastry Mastery

Filo, or phyllo pastry, is one of the most delicate and versatile ingredients in the pastry world. Known for its tissue-thin sheets that crisp to golden perfection, filo is the cornerstone of many iconic recipes, from savory Spanakopita to sweet apple strudel and layered baklava. While working with filo pastry can be challenging due to its fragility, mastering its techniques opens up a world of culinary possibilities.

In this chapter, we will explore the art of working with filo pastry, share detailed recipes for three beloved dishes, and provide expert tips for handling, storing, and preparing this unique dough.

Understanding Filo Pastry

Filo pastry consists of paper-thin layers of unleavened dough, typically made from flour, water, and a small amount of oil or vinegar. These sheets are stretched until they are nearly transparent, creating a versatile base for both sweet and savory dishes.

1. Characteristics of Filo Pastry

- Fragility: Filo sheets are extremely thin and tear easily, requiring careful handling.

- Crisp Texture: When baked, the layers puff slightly and develop a crisp, flaky texture.

- Neutral Flavor: Filo pastry has a mild taste, making it suitable for a wide range of flavor profiles.

2. Key Tips for Success

1. Work Quickly: Filo sheets dry out rapidly when exposed to air. Always cover unused sheets with a damp kitchen towel.

2. Use Plenty of Butter or Oil: Brushing each sheet with melted butter or oil helps create the signature flakiness and ensures the layers adhere.

3. Layer Strategically: Multiple layers add stability and enhance texture, especially for fillings that release moisture during baking.

4. Trim Carefully: Use a sharp knife or scissors to cut filo to the desired size, avoiding tearing.

Recipes

1. Spanakopita

Spanakopita is a classic Greek savory pastry filled with spinach, feta cheese, and herbs, encased in crisp, golden filo sheets.

Ingredients (Serves 6):

- 1 package filo pastry, thawed
    - 1/2 cup (115 g) unsalted butter, melted
    - 1 pound (450 g) fresh spinach, washed and chopped
    - 1/2 cup (100 g) feta cheese, crumbled
    - 1/4 cup (25 g) grated Parmesan cheese
    - 1 small onion, finely chopped
    - 2 cloves garlic, minced
    - 2 tablespoons fresh dill, chopped
    - 2 eggs, beaten
    - Salt and pepper to taste

Instructions:

1. Prepare the Filling:

- In a skillet, sauté onion and garlic until fragrant. Add spinach and cook until wilted. Drain excess liquid and cool.

- Mix the spinach with feta, Parmesan, dill, eggs, salt, and pepper.

2. Layer the Filo:

- Preheat the oven to 375°F (190°C). Brush a baking dish with melted butter. Layer 6 filo sheets in the dish, brushing each with butter.

3. Add the Filling:

- Spread the spinach mixture evenly over the filo. Cover with 6 more filo sheets, brushing each with butter.

4. Bake:

- Trim any overhanging pastry and bake for 30–35 minutes, or until golden and crisp. Cool slightly before slicing.

2. Apple Strudel

This Austrian classic features a spiced apple filling wrapped in layers of filo dough, baked to a golden crisp.

Ingredients (Serves 4):

- 6 sheets filo pastry, thawed
    - 1/2 cup (115 g) unsalted butter, melted
    - 4 medium apples, peeled and thinly sliced
    - 1/2 cup (100 g) granulated sugar
    - 1 teaspoon cinnamon
    - 1/4 teaspoon nutmeg
    - 1/4 cup (30 g) raisins (optional)
    - 1/4 cup (30 g) chopped walnuts or almonds (optional)
    - 1/4 cup (30 g) breadcrumbs

Instructions:

1. Prepare the Filling:

- In a bowl, mix apples, sugar, cinnamon, nutmeg, raisins, and nuts.

2. Layer the Filo:

- Preheat the oven to 375°F (190°C). Lay one sheet of filo on a work surface and brush with melted butter. Repeat with remaining sheets, stacking them.

3. Assemble the Strudel:

- Sprinkle breadcrumbs over the filo stack, leaving a 2-inch border. Spread the apple mixture on top. Fold in the edges and roll the strudel tightly.

4. Bake:

- Place the strudel seam-side down on a baking sheet. Brush with butter and bake for 30–35 minutes, or until golden. Cool before slicing.

3. Layered Baklava

Baklava is a rich, sweet pastry made of layers of filo, nuts, and syrup. This Middle Eastern favorite is a celebration of texture and flavor.

Ingredients (Serves 8):

For the Pastry:
- 1 package filo pastry, thawed
- 1 cup (225 g) unsalted butter, melted
- 2 cups (250 g) chopped walnuts or pistachios
- 1/4 cup (50 g) granulated sugar
- 1 teaspoon cinnamon
For the Syrup:
- 1 cup (200 g) sugar
- 1/2 cup (120 ml) honey
- 1/2 cup (120 ml) water
- 1 teaspoon rosewater or orange blossom water (optional)

Instructions:

1. Prepare the Syrup:
- In a saucepan, combine sugar, honey, and water. Simmer for 10 minutes. Add rosewater if using. Cool completely.
   2. Layer the Filo:
- Preheat the oven to 350°F (175°C). Brush a 9x13-inch pan with butter. Layer 8 filo sheets, brushing each with butter. Sprinkle a thin layer of nuts mixed with sugar and cinnamon. Repeat until all ingredients are used, finishing with 8 layers of filo.
   3. Cut and Bake:
- Use a sharp knife to cut the baklava into diamonds or squares. Bake for 45–50 minutes, or until golden and crisp.

4. Add Syrup:

- Pour cooled syrup over the hot baklava. Let soak for several hours before serving.

Tips for Handling and Storing Filo Dough

1. Handling Filo Dough

- Thaw Properly: Defrost frozen filo in the refrigerator overnight.

- Use a Damp Towel: Cover unused filo sheets with a slightly damp towel to prevent drying.

- Work Quickly: Assemble dishes efficiently to minimize handling time.

2. Storing Filo Dough

- Refrigeration: Wrap unused filo tightly in plastic wrap and store in the refrigerator for up to 1 week.

- Freezing: Re-freeze unused filo by wrapping it tightly and storing it in the freezer for up to 2 months.

3. Repairing Tears

- Small tears in filo sheets can be patched with an extra layer of filo or brushed with butter to seal.

Conclusion

Filo pastry is a versatile and rewarding ingredient that adds elegance and texture to both sweet and savory dishes. By mastering the techniques for handling filo and experimenting with recipes like Spanakopita, apple strudel, and baklava, you can elevate your pastry-making skills to new heights. With its crisp layers and rich flavor, filo pastry is sure to impress at any table.

In the next chapter, we'll delve into *"Modern Pastry Innovations,"* exploring creative techniques and contemporary recipes to push the boundaries of traditional pastry-making. Let's continue!

Chapter 14: Decorative Techniques

Pastry-making is as much an art as it is a science. While flavors and textures are undeniably important, the visual appeal of a pastry can elevate it from delicious to unforgettable. Decorative techniques like braiding, latticework, and stenciling transform pastries into stunning centerpieces that impress before the first bite.

This chapter dives into advanced decorative techniques, including braiding and latticework for crusts, using stencils and cutters for intricate designs, and incorporating natural dyes to add vibrant colors. You'll also learn how to create show-stopping pastry centerpieces that steal the spotlight at any gathering.

The Importance of Decoration in Pastry

A well-decorated pastry doesn't just look beautiful—it reflects the baker's attention to detail and elevates the dining experience.

- First Impressions: A stunning pastry draws people in and creates excitement about what's inside.

- Creative Expression: Decoration allows bakers to showcase their personality and artistic flair.

- Special Occasions: Elaborate designs make pastries memorable for holidays, weddings, and other celebrations.

Key Tools for Decorative Pastry Work

- Pastry Cutters: Create uniform shapes for lattices, cutouts, and embellishments.

- Embossing Tools: Add texture and patterns to dough.

- Pastry Stencils: Achieve intricate designs using powdered sugar, cocoa, or edible sprays.

- Natural Dyes: Use ingredients like beet juice, turmeric, and spinach to color dough.

- Egg Wash Brushes: Apply an even egg wash for a golden finish that enhances designs.

Decorative Crust Techniques

The crust is the canvas of a pastry. From braiding to latticework, there are countless ways to enhance its visual appeal.

1. Braiding

Braiding dough adds texture and sophistication to pastry edges. This technique is perfect for pies, tarts, and braided bread.

How to Braid Dough:

1. Roll out the dough into a thin sheet and cut it into long strips, about 1/4 inch wide.

2. Group three strips together and pinch the ends to secure them.

3. Cross the outer strips over the middle strip alternately to form a braid.

4. Attach the braid to the edge of a pie or tart, pressing gently to adhere.

Tips for Success:

- Keep the dough chilled to prevent stretching or tearing.

- Use even pressure while braiding to create uniform thickness.

2. Latticework

Latticework is a timeless decoration for fruit pies, allowing the filling to peek through while adding structural support.

How to Create a Lattice Top:

1. Roll out the dough and cut it into strips, about 1/2 inch wide.

2. Lay half the strips horizontally across the pie, leaving equal spacing between them.

3. Fold back alternate strips and lay one strip vertically across the pie. Return the folded strips to their original position.

4. Repeat the process, alternating strips to weave a lattice pattern. Trim and seal the edges.

Tips for Success:

- Use a ruler for straight, even strips.
  - Brush the lattice with egg wash to enhance its golden color.

3. Cutouts and Appliqués

Using cutouts is an easy way to add intricate designs to pie tops or tart edges.

How to Create Cutouts:

1. Roll out the dough and use small cutters (e.g., leaves, stars, flowers) to cut shapes.

2. Arrange the cutouts on top of the pastry, overlapping them for added dimension.

3. Adhere the cutouts with a small amount of water or egg wash.

Tips for Success:

- Freeze cutouts for a few minutes before transferring to prevent stretching.
  - Combine different shapes for a dynamic design.

Using Stencils, Cutters, and Dyes

1. Stenciling

Stenciling adds elegant patterns to pastries using powdered sugar, cocoa, or edible sprays.

How to Stencil Pastry:

1. Place a stencil on the baked pastry.
   2. Lightly dust with powdered sugar or cocoa using a fine mesh sieve.
   3. Carefully lift the stencil to reveal the design.

Tips for Success:

- Use stencils with bold patterns for maximum impact.
   - Ensure the pastry is cool before applying the stencil to prevent melting.

2. Using Natural Dyes

Natural dyes add color without artificial ingredients, perfect for themed pastries.

Sources for Natural Dyes:

- Red: Beet juice or pomegranate juice
   - Yellow: Turmeric or saffron
   - Green: Spinach puree or matcha powder
   - Purple: Blueberry or blackberry juice

How to Use Natural Dyes:

1. Mix the dye into the dough or brush it onto the surface before baking.
   2. Combine colors for ombre or marbled effects.

Tips for Success:

- Start with a small amount of dye to control intensity.
   - Use concentrated juices for vibrant colors.

Creating Show-Stopping Pastry Centerpieces

Centerpieces like croquembouche towers, galette wreaths, and intricate braided breads make a bold statement at any gathering.

1. Croquembouche Tower

A traditional French dessert, croquembouche consists of cream-filled choux pastries stacked into a cone and bound with caramel.

How to Assemble a Croquembouche:

1. Prepare cream puffs filled with pastry cream or whipped cream.

2. Dip each puff into caramel and stack them in a cone shape on a serving platter.

3. Drizzle additional caramel over the tower for a glossy finish.

2. Galette Wreath

A galette wreath is a rustic yet elegant pastry shaped into a circular form with overlapping layers.

How to Make a Galette Wreath:

1. Roll out the dough into a large circle and spread the filling (e.g., spiced fruit or savory vegetables) in a ring around the center.

2. Fold the outer edges of the dough over the filling, overlapping to create a wreath shape.

3. Bake until golden and garnish with fresh herbs or powdered sugar.

3. Braided Bread Loaf

A braided bread loaf combines artistry with delicious flavor, ideal for special occasions.

How to Braid Bread Dough:

1. Divide the dough into three equal portions and roll each into a long rope.

2. Pinch the ends together and braid the ropes.

3. Tuck the ends under the loaf and brush with egg wash before baking.

Pro Tips for Decorative Pastry Success

1. Plan Ahead: Sketch your design before starting to ensure a cohesive look.

2. Use Chilled Dough: Cold dough is easier to shape and holds its form during baking.

3. Practice Makes Perfect: Experiment with techniques on scrap dough before applying them to your final pastry.

4. Incorporate Texture: Use tools like forks, knives, or embossing mats to add texture to dough surfaces.

5. Balance Simplicity and Complexity: A well-executed simple design can be just as impactful as a more intricate one.

Conclusion

Decorative techniques like braiding, latticework, and stenciling transform pastries into edible works of art. By mastering these methods and incorporating tools like cutters, stencils, and natural dyes, you can elevate your baking to a professional level. Whether creating an intricate croquembouche or a rustic galette wreath, these skills allow you to craft pastries that are as beautiful as they are delicious.

In the final chapter, we'll explore *"The Joy of Sharing Pastry,"* reflecting on the cultural significance of baking and how it brings people together. Let's wrap up this pastry journey with inspiration and celebration!

Chapter 15: Gluten-Free and Vegan Pastries

In recent years, the demand for gluten-free and vegan pastries has grown significantly, driven by dietary restrictions, health-conscious lifestyles, and a desire for inclusivity in baking. Creating gluten-free and vegan pastries that are as delicious and satisfying as their traditional counterparts can seem challenging, but with the right techniques, ingredients, and a little creativity, it's entirely possible to achieve extraordinary results.

This chapter explores how to adapt traditional pastry recipes for special diets, provides detailed recipes for gluten-free tart crust, vegan puff pastry, and dairy-free choux, and offers tips for maintaining the texture, flavor, and structure that make pastries so delightful.

Understanding Gluten-Free and Vegan Baking

Gluten and dairy play key roles in traditional pastry-making, so replacing them requires a solid understanding of their functions and suitable substitutes.

1. Gluten-Free Baking

The Role of Gluten

- Gluten, found in wheat, barley, and rye, provides elasticity and structure in dough. It helps trap air, giving pastries their light, airy texture.

Gluten-Free Flours

Replacing wheat flour is one of the biggest challenges in gluten-free baking. Here are some common options:
- Almond Flour: Adds moisture and a slightly nutty flavor, excellent for tart crusts.

- Rice Flour: A neutral-flavored flour that works well in blends.
- Tapioca Starch: Provides elasticity and chewiness.
- Xanthan Gum or Psyllium Husk: Mimics gluten's binding properties in gluten-free doughs.

2. Vegan Baking

Challenges of Vegan Pastries

Traditional pastries rely heavily on butter, milk, and eggs for richness, structure, and leavening. Vegan alternatives must replicate these qualities.

Vegan Substitutes

- Butter Alternatives: Coconut oil, margarine, or vegan butter provide similar fat content.
- Milk Alternatives: Almond milk, oat milk, or soy milk work well in most recipes.
- Egg Replacements: Flaxseed meal, chia seeds, or commercial egg replacers can substitute eggs in binding and leavening.

Recipes

1. Gluten-Free Tart Crust

A gluten-free tart crust can be the base for sweet or savory dishes, with a flaky texture and rich flavor.

Ingredients (For 1 Tart):

- 1 1/4 cups (150 g) almond flour
- 1/2 cup (60 g) tapioca starch
- 1/4 cup (50 g) coconut oil or vegan butter, melted
- 1 tablespoon ground flaxseed mixed with 3 tablespoons water (flax egg)

- 1/4 teaspoon salt

Instructions:

1. Prepare the Flax Egg:

- Mix ground flaxseed with water and let sit for 5 minutes to thicken.

2. Combine Ingredients:

- In a bowl, mix almond flour, tapioca starch, salt, melted coconut oil, and the flax egg until a dough forms.

3. Chill the Dough:

- Shape the dough into a disc, wrap it in plastic wrap, and refrigerate for 30 minutes.

4. Roll Out and Bake:

- Preheat the oven to 350°F (175°C). Roll the dough between two sheets of parchment paper and fit it into a tart pan.

- Bake for 15–20 minutes, or until lightly golden. Let cool before filling.

2. Vegan Puff Pastry

Creating vegan puff pastry requires patience, but the results are worth the effort. This recipe uses vegan butter for flaky layers.

Ingredients (Makes 1 Sheet):

- 2 1/2 cups (315 g) all-purpose flour or gluten-free flour blend
- 1 teaspoon salt
- 1/2 cup (120 ml) cold water
- 1 cup (225 g) vegan butter, chilled and cubed

Instructions:

1. Prepare the Dough:

- Mix flour and salt in a bowl. Add water gradually, mixing until the dough comes together. Chill for 30 minutes.

2. Incorporate the Butter:

- Roll the dough into a 12x6-inch rectangle. Place the cubed butter in the center and fold the dough over it like an envelope. Chill for 20 minutes.

3. Laminate the Dough:

- Roll the dough into a rectangle, then fold it into thirds. Repeat the process four times, chilling between each fold.

4. Use as Needed:

- Roll out and cut the dough as required for your recipe. Bake at 400°F (200°C) until golden and crisp.

3. Dairy-Free Choux Pastry

Choux pastry, used for éclairs and cream puffs, can be adapted for a dairy-free diet without sacrificing its light, airy texture.

Ingredients (Makes 12 Puffs):

- 1/2 cup (120 ml) water
    - 1/2 cup (120 ml) almond milk
    - 1/2 cup (115 g) vegan butter
    - 1 cup (125 g) all-purpose flour or gluten-free flour blend
    - 4 tablespoons aquafaba (liquid from canned chickpeas)

Instructions:

1. Make the Dough:

- In a saucepan, heat water, almond milk, and vegan butter until boiling. Add the flour all at once and stir until the dough pulls away from the sides of the pan.

2. Incorporate Aquafaba:

- Remove from heat and let cool slightly. Beat in the aquafaba one tablespoon at a time until the dough is smooth and glossy.

3. Shape and Bake:

- Pipe the dough onto a parchment-lined baking sheet. Bake at 375°F (190°C) for 25–30 minutes, or until golden and hollow inside.

4. Fill:

- Cool completely before filling with vegan pastry cream or coconut whipped cream.

Tips for Maintaining Texture and Flavor

Creating gluten-free and vegan pastries requires extra attention to ensure they're as satisfying as traditional versions.

1. Achieving Flakiness

- Use chilled fats and handle the dough minimally to prevent melting.

- Add a bit of cornstarch or tapioca starch to gluten-free dough for elasticity.

2. Adding Richness

- Incorporate nuts, seeds, or coconut milk for richness without dairy.

- Toast gluten-free flours lightly to deepen their flavor.

3. Avoiding Crumbliness

- Use xanthan gum or psyllium husk to bind gluten-free dough.

- Let dough rest after mixing to hydrate and develop structure.

4. Enhancing Flavor

- Increase the use of flavor enhancers like spices, citrus zest, or extracts to compensate for subtle differences in alternative flours and fats.

Common Challenges and Solutions

1. Dry Dough

- Problem: Gluten-free and vegan doughs can be dry or crumbly.

- Solution: Add small amounts of water or plant-based milk until the dough comes together.

2. Soggy Crusts

- Problem: Alternative flours absorb moisture differently, leading to soggy crusts.

- Solution: Pre-bake (blind bake) crusts and use moisture-resistant fillings.

3. Dense Texture

- Problem: Gluten-free and vegan pastries can feel heavy.

- Solution: Use leaveners like baking powder or aquafaba to lighten the texture.

Conclusion

Gluten-free and vegan pastries are no longer an afterthought—they can be just as indulgent, flaky, and delicious as traditional ones. By mastering the techniques for alternative flours, fats, and binders, you can create pastries that accommodate dietary needs without compromising flavor or texture. Recipes like gluten-free tart crust, vegan puff pastry, and dairy-free choux pastry showcase the possibilities for innovation in the world of special-diet baking.

In this chapter, we've explored how to make pastry inclusive for everyone. As this book concludes, remember that the joy of baking lies in experimentation, creativity, and sharing your creations with others. Let your pastry journey continue with confidence and inspiration!

Conclusion: Your Pastry Journey

Pastry-making is a beautiful blend of science, art, and tradition. Over the course of this book, we've explored the techniques, recipes, and inspiration needed to master the art of pastry. From crafting the perfect crust to creating show-stopping desserts and adapting recipes for dietary needs, your pastry journey has been one of growth, experimentation, and discovery.

This chapter serves as both a recap and a call to action. Pastry-making is not just about following recipes—it's about creativity, connection, and the joy of sharing your creations with others. Whether you're a beginner or a seasoned baker, your journey with pastries is only just beginning.

Recap: Mastering the Foundations

The Importance of Technique

The foundation of great pastry lies in technique. The ability to create tender crusts, fluffy doughs, and perfectly layered pastries depends on understanding the processes and practicing them consistently.

Key Techniques Recap:

1. Perfecting Doughs:
    - Mastered shortcrust, puff pastry, filo, and choux pastry techniques.
    - Learned how to laminate doughs for flakiness and handle delicate sheets for precision.
    2. Layering and Filling:
    - Explored the art of filling pastries with creams, curds, fruits, and savory ingredients.
    - Balanced textures and flavors to enhance every bite.
    3. Decorative Skills:
    - Gained confidence in latticework, braiding, and stenciling to create stunning visuals.

- Used natural dyes, cutouts, and embossing tools to make pastries stand out.

A World of Pastry Creations

From simple classics to elaborate showpieces, this book has provided recipes and techniques to suit every skill level and occasion.

Recipe Highlights:

- Sweet Pastries:
    - Fruit pies, chocolate tarts, and creamy éclairs.
    - Laminated favorites like croissants and Danish pastries.
    - Savory Pastries:
    - Quiches, pot pies, and hand pies perfect for meals or appetizers.
    - Global influences like spanakopita, empanadas, and meat pies.
    - Special Diets:
    - Gluten-free tart crusts, vegan puff pastry, and dairy-free choux pastries.
    - Techniques to ensure texture, flavor, and inclusivity in every bite.

Encouragement to Experiment

Pastry as a Creative Outlet

Pastry-making is not just about following instructions—it's about experimentation and personalization. Every recipe is a starting point, inviting you to add your own flair and adapt it to your taste.

Ways to Experiment:

1. Flavors:
    - Infuse your doughs and fillings with unique spices, herbs, or extracts.
    - Pair unexpected ingredients, like lavender and lemon or chili and chocolate.
    2. Textures:
    - Play with crunch, creaminess, and chewiness to create dynamic pastries.

- Add nuts, seeds, or candied fruit for contrast.
3. Designs:
- Develop your own decorative techniques, from braided edges to intricate stencils.
- Experiment with color using natural dyes or edible paints.

Learning from Mistakes

Every baker, no matter how experienced, faces challenges. A crust might shrink, a puff pastry might not rise, or a filling might curdle. These moments are opportunities to learn and refine your skills.

Tips for Growth:

- Analyze Your Results: Reflect on what went wrong and how you can adjust next time.
- Seek Inspiration: Look to other bakers, books, and cultural traditions for fresh ideas.
- Keep Practicing: The more you bake, the more intuitive and skilled you'll become.

The Joy of Sharing Pastries

Pastry-making is inherently communal. From the kitchen to the dining table, it fosters connection, celebration, and delight.

Creating Memories

Pastries have the power to evoke memories and create new ones. A birthday cake, a holiday tart, or a simple pie shared with friends becomes part of a story.

Examples of Pastry Moments:

- Family Traditions: Recreating recipes passed down through generations.
- Celebrations: Marking milestones with intricately decorated pastries.

- Everyday Joys: Bringing people together over a warm batch of croissants or a flaky galette.

Inspiring Others

Sharing pastries isn't just about serving them—it's about inspiring others to join in the journey. Encourage friends and family to bake with you or try their hand at pastry-making.

Ways to Inspire:

- Host Baking Days: Invite loved ones to join you in the kitchen.
    - Share Your Recipes: Pass on your creations and adaptations to others.
    - Teach and Mentor: Help new bakers gain confidence and skills.

Your Pastry Journey Continues

A Lifelong Love for Pastry

Pastry-making is a skill that evolves over time. As you continue to practice, experiment, and share your creations, your confidence and repertoire will grow. Embrace the challenges, celebrate the successes, and enjoy the process.

Final Thoughts

Pastries are more than just food—they're expressions of love, creativity, and joy. They bring people together, create memories, and add beauty to everyday life. By mastering the techniques and recipes in this book, you've gained the foundation to explore the endless possibilities of pastry-making.

As you continue your journey, remember that every pastry tells a story. Let your creativity and passion shine through in every crust, filling, and decoration. Most importantly, savor the moments of connection and celebration that come with sharing your creations.

Here's to a lifetime of delicious, beautiful pastries and the joy they bring to your life and the lives of those around you.

Happy baking!

Don't miss out!

Visit the website below and you can sign up to receive emails whenever Olivia Bennett publishes a new book. There's no charge and no obligation.

https://books2read.com/r/B-A-QLEKD-JOMAG

BOOKS2READ

Connecting independent readers to independent writers.

About the Author

Olivia Bennett is a celebrated food writer and chef with expertise spanning multiple culinary disciplines. With a passion for making home cooking accessible, she specializes in guiding readers through everything from hearty casseroles to delicate pastries. Her work is known for its clear instructions, practical tips, and deep understanding of both traditional and modern cooking techniques.